To Pat
From Woods

grasses
pods
vines
weeds

grasses pods vines weeds
Decorating with Texas Naturals
BY QUENTIN STEITZ

UNIVERSITY OF TEXAS PRESS, AUSTIN

TO MY FAMILY
Frank Pierce Steitz
and
Robin Win Steitz

Copyright © 1987
by University of Texas Press
All rights reserved
Printed in Japan

First Edition, 1987

Requests for permission to reproduce material from this work should be sent to Permissions, University of Texas Press, Box 7819, Austin, Texas 78713-7819.

Library of Congress Cataloging-in-Publication Data

Steitz, Quentin, 1924–
   Grasses, pods, vines, weeds.

  Bibliography: p.
  Includes index.
  1. Plants—Collection and preservation.
2. Plants, Ornamental—Texas—Collection and preservation. 3. Botany—Texas.
4. Flower arrangement. 5. Dried flower arrangement. 6. Wild flower gardening—Texas. I. Title.
SB447.S74 1987   747′.98   86-19209
ISBN 0-292-78086-9

Contents

ACKNOWLEDGMENTS AND PHOTOGRAPHY vii

INTRODUCTION 1

TEXAS AND NATURALS 2

grasses
- Virginia Wild Rye 6
- Canada Wild Rye 8
- Perennial Ryegrass 10
- Johnson Grass 12
- Foxtail Millet 14
- Wild and Common Oat 16
- Purple Three-awn 18
- Little Bluestem 20
- Broadleaf Uniola 22
- Southwest Bristle Grass 24
- Giant Reed 26
- Japanese Brome 28
- Purpletop 30
- Indian Grass 32
- Splitbeard Bluestem 34

pods
- Macartney Rose 38
- Mexican Hat 40
- Wild Onion 42
- American Lotus 44
- Black-eyed Susan 46
- Horsemint 48
- Silverleaf Nightshade 50
- Western Soapberry 52
- Tree of Heaven 54
- Bois d'Arc 56
- Retama 58
- Chinaberry 60
- Eastern Cottonwood 62
- Red Buckeye 64
- American Sycamore 66
- Dwarf Palmetto 68

vines
- Alamo Vine 72
- Old-Man's-Beard 74
- Common Trumpet Creeper 76
- Pepper Vine 78
- Rattan Vine 80
- Japanese Honeysuckle 82
- Carolina Snailseed 84

weeds
- Woolly Croton 88
- Common Broomweed 90
- Curly Dock 92
- Bagpod Sesbania 94
- Narrowleaf Cattail 96
- Horsetail 98

NATURAL TECHNIQUES 101

CULTIVATION AND CONSERVATION 108

GLOSSARY 118

REFERENCES 120

INDEX 121

Acknowledgments and Photography

The past twelve years spent in the development of natural vegetation for designing have brought me in contact with many people who encouraged me to further the idea that this is an important decorative field. Friends, educators, and designers have lent their experience, knowledge, and inspiration in writing this book. I sincerely thank the following persons:

Katy Seymour of Columbus, a friend who with me recognized the beauty of the so-called common grasses, flowers, and weeds gathered during my earliest experimentation. It was she who gave me the opportunity on many occasions to design and demonstrate the naturals of Colorado County to the garden clubs of the area.

Leonard Tharp, James Bailey, and Charles Thomas of Houston were the first designers to accept my introduction of new natural vegetation for creative floral designing. Leonard Tharp has shown his generosity for many years in aiding me and others in this field by sharing his expertise.

Katch Bacheller, James Bailey, James Browning, Kathy Burris, Mieko Cooper, Linnie Harris, Maggie Herbert, Scott Jenkins, James Kana, Clif Lotspeich, Kathryn Miller, Rex Minyard, Robert Palmer, Lyman Ratcliffe, Mark Ruisinger, Anna Schindler, Leonard Tharp, Charles Thomas, and Joe Wilson—their contribution of arrangements specifically designed for the photographs in Chapter 2 and the creativity displayed in using natural materials are greatly appreciated.

Celestine Gully, Charlie Gray of Frelsburg, Kathy Burris and Jerry Hargrove of Columbus, and Dorothy Mikulencak of Georgetown are those who assisted me in long hours of gathering in the field during both beautiful and miserable days. To Celestine, who learned to pick cotton as a child, I owe more than I can repay for her many dedicated hours. It was refreshing to observe her fascination with and developing awareness for the uncultivated species.

Gay Elliott McFarland of Houston, in her article in the *Houston Chronicle* about my use of decorative plants, made me realize that this subject is of interest to a wide cross section of people. This interest helped to formulate my idea to write on the beautiful decorative plants of Texas.

James L. Johnson, director of the Benz School of Floral Design, Texas A&M University, because of his appreciation of Texas dried vegetation, inspired me to further explore plants for designing and to write a book on the subject.

Dr. B. L. Turner, director of the Plant Resources Center, University of Texas at Austin, through his kindness gave generously of his expert advice on the usage of botanical words and identification of species.

Rupert D. Palmer, extension weed specialist, Texas Agricultural Extension Service, Texas A&M University, was of invaluable assistance in answering many questions, especially in weed identification. His interest and comments were of encouragement to me.

Mary Sanger, Marketing Department, Texas Department of Agriculture, through her work to preserve Texas native plants gave me a better understanding of the endless hours and tedious work involved in writing this book.

My friend Mary McCausland of Columbus, whose wit, sense of humor, and insight have been a blessing at difficult times. Her keen understanding of words helped me through my first trying days in finding words and phrases to express my ideas.

I would be remiss if I omitted a thank you to all ranchers and landowners of Colorado, Austin, and Williamson counties who allowed me access to their property in scouting and gathering.

Photography has been selected to capture the growth stages of the natural vegetation. In some species, particularly grasses, transition occurs rapidly due to climatic conditions and the resulting growth patterns are noticeable. In observing naturals, on a day-to-day basis, photography illustrates the details from early stages through maturity. There were frustrating hours of waiting for favorable conditions, and I appreciate the tenacity and the patience of those working with me in obtaining these photographs:

Gibbs Milliken, Art Department of the University of Texas at Austin, is responsible for almost all the photographs of the designs, and many field shots.

Don Berkman, free-lance photographer of Austin, is credited with most of the outdoor photographs depicting growth stages.

Diane Young, photographer of Houston, provided additional images of designs and all of the outdoor photographs of the American lotus.

In order to provide specific credit, the above-named photographers' initials have been included in the descriptions of the photographs.

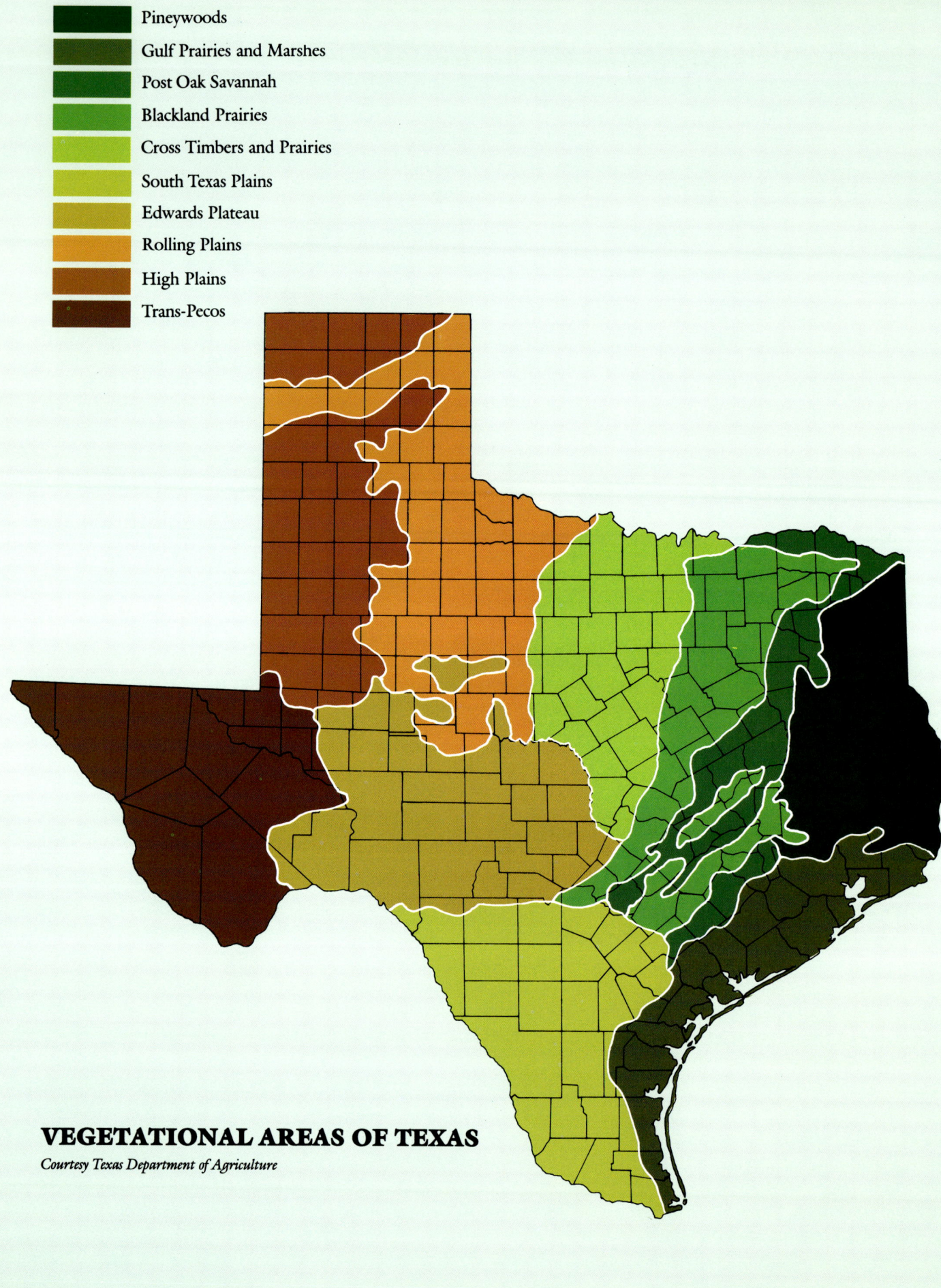

Introduction

This book is intended to enhance the reader's knowledge and appreciation of the use of native and naturalized Texas plants in decorative design and beautification. It describes and illustrates how to recognize, cultivate, prepare, and utilize native and naturalized species. The material presented here should be of assistance to garden club members in introducing new plant life for their design and conservation projects. The book should inspire designers with a new approach in the use of materials that have not been fully explored in the floral industry. It can be used as a handbook for schools of design, craftspersons, study groups, and homemakers and to increase ranchers' appreciation of decorative grasses. To those who enjoy Texas' natural surroundings, these words and photographs can supply additional hours of pleasure in the wonderment of nature.

The application of natural materials is leading to a new concept in design. The increased appreciation and use of ornamental plant life in designing is exciting imaginations and promoting creativity. Partly due to a lack of awareness of its great potential in beautification, plant life often has been neglected. However, government and private organizations are encouraging landscapers to become conscious of materials in the open fields. The Texas Highway Department has been successful for the past fifty years in promoting highway beautification—for instance, mowing and subsequent broadcasting of wild flowers and grasses.

Consider what has made Texas aesthetically outstanding: the magnificent vegetation, especially grasses and wild flowers, that graces the valleys, prairies, hills, and coastal areas. The public is becoming more aware of Texas' bounty. Such awareness will further the cultivation and preservation of many of the rarer native and decorative naturalized species. As natural materials become more popular, the demand can be increasingly supplied by professional harvesters, landscapers, commercial growers, and seed suppliers. A strong effort must be maintained to encourage the cultivation of native plants, for constant reaping without sowing will bring about the depletion of much of our living beauty.

Texas has been divided into ten vegetational areas based on topographic, climatic, and soil factors: Pineywoods, Gulf Prairies and Marshes, Post Oak Savannah, Blackland Prairies, Cross Timbers and Prairies, South Texas Plains, Edwards Plateau, Rolling Plains, High Plains, and Trans-Pecos. These areas are used to locate the habitat of the species discussed here.

The plants shown in the photographs, except for the cultivated species, were selected, collected, prepared, and dried by me. The use of natural materials is illustrated in designs by nineteen designers, as well as my decorative examples. Over a period of two years, I spent hours in the field scouting plants for the three photographers.

Texas and Naturals

Since the days of the Republic, and even prior to that time, Texas has been an interesting field for research and observation by naturalists and botanists from all over the world.

Texas offers an abundance of plant life in great variety. Scientists have determined that there are more than 5,000 species of flowering plants in Texas, of which 523 are grasses. This state has more species than any other largely because of its size and considerable variations of climate, soil, and topographic conditions. Environmental conditions range from the subtropical Lower Gulf Coast to the desert and higher elevations of the Trans-Pecos.

Contributing ecological factors affecting Texas vegetation include weather, soil, and elevation conditions that provide habitat for the same species to grow in widely separated areas of the state. The enormous distances between such localities illustrate the vastness of Texas. It is typical to find a specific tree, such as the ornamental tamarisk, providing wildlife cover in extreme geographical points. This genus, also known as salt-cedar, grows in the Matagorda coastal area, thriving in the salt flats and marshes, and in the higher elevations of the Trans-Pecos on the banks of the Rio Grande.

The climatic zones in Texas have been characterized as arid, semiarid, humid, and subhumid. The annual rainfall is high in extreme East Texas, producing wet marshes, and becomes progressively less westward to the desert and mountain surroundings of El Paso.

Candelilla, or wax euphorbia, has an unusual ability to adapt to the arid zones of West Texas bordering Mexico. Producing a wax coating to control loss of plant liquid to the dry air, it has adapted to the desert environment. American lotus has adapted equally to the humidity of the Jasper and Toledo Bend waterways as to the lakes of semi-arid San Angelo. Throughout the state, Mexican hat can be found blooming during spring rains, although the cone part of this flower grows larger in the wetter sections of the state than in the dryer western areas. After dying back, the flower can rebloom wherever rainfall occurs during late summer and fall.

The average growing season is longest in the Lower Rio Grande Valley and shortest in the northwestern Panhandle. The gateway to the bluebonnet spring season is in the Valley in late February. Traveling northward, bluebonnets arrive in the North Central Prairie approximately two months later, depending on climatic conditions.

Noted for sudden changes of temperature, from excessive heat to severe freezes, Texas is known for its "blue northers." High winds occur in the northern High Plains, while South Central Texas has inconsistent winds. Native plants with a deep root system, such as little bluestem and Indian grass, can weather the erratic temperatures and lack of moisture that are common in the Panhandle and the Big Bend country.

A wide range of soil characteristics exists in the state, from the desert saline of the Trans-Pecos to the fertile lime of the Blackland Prairies to the sandy, infertile soils of the Pineywoods.

The Blacklands' rich, dark soils are renowned for fertility and are among Texas' most productive farmland. Although much of this area is under cultivation, meadows still exist with tall grass vegetation. Switch grass, big bluestem, splitbeard bluestem, Indian grass, little bluestem, and side oats grama are a few of the colorful grasses. Adding to the pictorial beauty of this area, these grasses are found growing in patches and fields on the oak-topped ridges, the gentle rolling hills, and the prairies.

The soils of the swamps, marshes, and bogs of the Pineywoods provide certain necessary conditions for some of the unusual plants of Texas. Flourishing in the dampness and acid soils, mayapple, jack-in-the-pulpit, sarracenia, yellow lady's slipper orchid, and swamp lily are indigenous to the area. Typical prairie vegetation restricted to clay sites includes Virginia wild rye, Canada wild rye, and purpletop, all of which are decorative grasses.

The Trans-Pecos area, due to its wide range of mountains, plateaus, and valleys, is diverse in habitat and vegetation. Soils in general are calcareous and in most areas alkaline. Characteristic range sites, developed from the outwash materials of the mountains, are clay flats, sands, stony hills, saline soils, uplands, gypsum flats, rocky mountains, and gravel. An example of the wide variety of plants found includes ponderosa pine, growing on some of the higher elevated slopes; yucca, pinyon pine, and juniper on lower mountain sides; and desert shrubs and cacti in the dry basins and valleys—making this area outstanding for its natural beauty.

Some of the southwestern and Rocky Mountain grasses are found in the Trans-Pecos area, while they are noticeably absent from other regions of Texas.

Texas naturals are defined as native and naturalized plants, and if properly utilized they will supply dry and fresh materials for design. Natives are considered those plants indigenous to an area and existing without cultivation. Naturalized species are plants that have been introduced into an area, have escaped cultivation, and have continued to reproduce. Decorative naturals are classified for design purposes into four categories: grasses, pods, vines, and weeds.

The concept of "natural" indicates that the preferred treatment of the vegetation does not utilize artificial coloring or preservatives. Techniques for drying specimens by a natural process, described in Chapter 3, aid in preserving their natural appearance. Recommended methods for collecting and preparing fresh flora are essential in retaining the plant's quality, characteristics, and beauty. For instance, curly dock has been a popular dry material. When utilized and prepared for fresh usage, this weed introduces a new concept. The brilliant lime green and texture of this tall decorative present a fresh, new look.

Naturals are proving their value because they are equally as beautiful and aesthetically interesting as many of the cultivated species. Many plants, however, do not contain the necessary properties for design. Naturals used here contain design qualities of form, color, line, and texture. Most of the vegetation described herein represents a group of materials that have been relatively unavailable for decorative use by the public. One reason is that they were previously unrecognized as valuable sources for design. For instance, a common definition of a weed is any undesirable, uncultivated plant. However, we are now acknowledging a place for weeds in creating decorative pieces. Considered a pest, the drifting, tumbling tumbleweed has been purposeful in reinforcing fences to barricade against blowing sands. Known also as "Tumbleweed" Russian thistle, this species can be utilized decoratively for Christmas creations. Horseapple and chinaberry fruit is easily available, but only recently has it been used for fresh designing. Because the bois d'arc grows so widely, it has long been used for hedges, fence posts, and carvings. The fruit is now being used as fresh centerpieces.

In order that Texas naturals may flourish in the design field, awareness of their dissemination and development is essential. With observation and study of naturals, knowledge and awareness of growth patterns will develop. At certain stages of growth, from early development to maturity, these species take on distinctly different appearances. The four stages important in selecting a natural for dry or fresh designing are early, just prior to prime, prime, and past prime. Because climatic conditions affect the development of plant life, being conscious of these effects is important in preparing to use natural material. The development of grasses and flowers can occur rapidly; the period in which to select the correct growth stage is limited to a few days. Developing awareness is the art of directing one's attention—the more one looks, the more one sees, and the more one sees, the more one is compelled to look.

grasses

Elymus virginicus   **VIRGINIA WILD RYE**

top, early stage. D.B.
bottom, prime seed heads. D.B.
opposite, design. G.M.

Early Stage Two wild ryes belonging to the same genus, *Elymus virginicus* and *E. canadensis,* are descriptively close and are worth comparing. Virginia wild rye, a native of Texas, rises from the ground to develop spikes before excessive heat occurs, as do Canada wild rye and perennial ryegrass. Virginia wild rye ascends showing very pointed and narrow green leaves without texture, flourishing during cool spring nights and in the shade of wooded areas. In development, the top leaf is exceptionally pointed and distinctly angled on the culm. It is at this section of the stem that the compact spike emerges from the sheath, accentuating the last leaf that embraces the formation to follow. Late March through May.

Prime Stage This species grows 2'–3' in height and is shorter than the Canada wild rye. Both have spikes similar in length, 3"–5". The form of Virginia wild rye consists of compact inflorescences, exhibiting sections of alternating spikelets appearing in tiers that are stiffly erect and remain straight with maturity, unlike the nodding heads of Canada wild rye. Shorter awns, the outstanding characteristic of this grass, differ from the extremely long awns of Canada wild rye. Color of seed heads and blades changes little from the original dark green of early growth, unless the specimen is found in open areas subject to direct sun, when color then becomes subdued with growth. April through early June.

Design Peacock feathers and Virginia wild rye comprise this colorful example. The greens of the dried wild grass match those of the feathers. Virginia wild rye has both height and texture. Upward movement is directed by the stiff and erect heads at different heights and is in good contrast with the round and soft shapes of the downward plumes. Short and straight bristles of the rye deserve interest in comparison to the long and silky feathers, supplying elegant airiness around the edges of the display. A vibrant blue container has been selected to complement the peacock blues. Virginia wild rye is a species easily dried and renders a soft green in dried materials.

Notes of Interest Virginia wild rye is frequently planted in winter pastures and hay fields for its nutrition. A hardy species, it can be found growing in the United States from the Rocky Mountains eastward and into sections of Canada. Indigenous to Texas, this grass grows abundantly in rich moist lowlands in the eastern half of the state. It can be found throughout Texas, rarely in the High Plains and the Trans-Pecos areas. Perennial.

Elymus canadensis   **CANADA WILD RYE**

top, early stage. D.B.
bottom, nodding seed heads. D.B.
opposite, design. G.M.

Early Stage Canada wild rye is one of the prettiest and most desirable decorative native grasses, with similarities to Virginia wild rye. Its early leaf development can be identified by spear-like blades. The top leaf typically angled allows the beginning formation of the spike to protrude. Tightly enclosed in the sheath, the first evidence of the spike, are many awns projecting straight upward. Mid March through May.

Prime Stage Leaves develop 10"–14" in length and are widely spaced along the stem, rather than developing from the base. Culms grow 2'–4' in height, unusually thin, curving downward with the weight of fully developed inflorescences, as opposed to the erectness of Virginia wild rye. The distinguishing characteristics of this grass are the silky, luxurious heads that are fully developed at prime. The long awns are twice the length of an individual spikelet, considerably longer than those of the Virginia wild rye. Visually, this also doubles the volume. April through June.

Design The beauty of this grass lies in the voluminous and lustrous inflorescences. This dried example displays the decorative qualities in its use as a fine natural filler. Horned beak rush is introduced with curled leaves that have dried to the color of Canada wild rye. The round pods of Mexican buckeye supply an accent correlating the slip design of the vase.

Notes of Interest The fact that this species is usually found in colonies in protected areas, along roadsides and fence lines, is an indication that it is decreasing in the wild. It prefers shade, where stronger and more beautiful specimens are produced. It is of interest that this wild rye will hybridize with Virginia wild rye of the area. There are varieties of Canada wild rye in northerly regions, including southern Alaska; however, it has been established that the Texas plants have a separate origin. They are generally found throughout the state, rarely in parts of the South Texas Plains. A vernacular name, nodding wild rye, comes from the typical nodding heads. Perennial.

Lolium perenne

PERENNIAL RYEGRASS

top, early stage. D.B.
bottom, prime spikes. D.B.
opposite, design. G.M.

Early Stage Perennial ryegrass, a cool-weather grass, is commonly seen in early spring along roadsides and shoulders of major highways. Prominent markings of ear-shaped appendages occur on the stem at the leaf collar. Leaves, particularly thin and slender, develop inconspicuously on short culms. Spikelets are found with and without awns. The fresh green compact spikes are characteristically tinted slightly with purple on the outer edges of the spikelets. Late February through April.

Prime Stage There is relatively little change in appearance from early to prime, except in height the rickrack pattern is more clearly defined. Erect inflorescences reach above the leaves and the grass grows 2′–3′ in height. Leaves become succulently dark green, prominently basal, but quickly respond to lack of rainfall and rising temperatures by shriveling and turning to yellow-green. The inflorescence of several flowered spikelets can be easily detected by their unusual fitting into a concave rachis. It is the angle of the spikelets, set edgewise, that creates an uncommon rickrack pattern the length of the stem. March through May.

Design This common grass, with its interesting pattern of angling spikelets, relates to the use of a decorative dried material. The example in a simple cylinder depicts ryegrass in different forms from two drying techniques. The vertical straight lines illustrate drying in a hanging position. The other form, gracefully folding downward over the edge of the container, demonstrates the standing position to achieve a molded curve. The two forms are an interesting contrast of line and form with a consistent likeness of materials in two different shapes.

Notes of Interest Perennial ryegrass, or ray grass, was cultivated as the first grass pasture in Europe. Introduced into the United States for wildlife and livestock grazing, it is now widespread, particularly in northern states. This ryegrass is found throughout Texas, the exception usually being in parts of the South Texas Plains and the Trans-Pecos. Perennial.

Sorghum halepense

JOHNSON GRASS

top, tassel-like. D.B.
bottom, prime seed heads. G.M.
opposite, design. G.M.

Early Stage Johnson grass, although naturalized to Texas, is extremely adaptable in becoming an abundant natural. Arising from creeping rhizomes, the smooth culms are usually thick in comparison to the thin stems of many decorative grasses. Early growth, 12″–16″ in height, produces many alternating smooth leaves. The distinct feature of the leaf blade is a midvein, obviously white. Underdeveloped spikelets are tassel-like creamy yellowish, existing at the top of erect culms reaching approximately 30″ in height at this stage. Spring, summer, and fall.

Prime Stage This species, at prime, is a tall leafy grass. Mature leaves are flat, to ¾″ wide in the middle and tapering to a distinct point. The height, depending on climatic conditions of the area, ranges 3′–6′. Purple splotches, caused by bacteria, can occur on the leaves. The flowering seed heads are large, open panicles with branchlets occasionally in whorls. The numerous spikelets, in turning beautiful shades of purple during spring and fall growth, render a full-bodied, decorative seed head. Past prime, the awns fall, leaving the inflorescence fuzzy and unattractive. Inflorescences of summer growth are almost always blonde in color. A warm season species whenever rainfall is adequate, fresh Johnson grass will appear in mowed areas. It is optional if leaves are pretty enough to be included as part of the design material or stripped to emphasize the spikes. This hardy grass is also durable when used fresh, lasting seven to ten days. It will tolerate lack of water, depending on temperatures, for a few hours after being allowed to absorb water when cut. Spring, summer, and fall.

Design Although commonplace, Johnson grass can be beautiful. An inventive floral shaft has been created here in an original use of fresh Johnson grass. The design includes blending together 350 stems of the grass, with foliage and flowering heads at various stages, and using fresh chinaberries and sunflowers, wild and cultivated. It is a work of art in the midst of nature—a true expression of a natural. Design by Leonard Tharp of Houston, Texas.

Notes of Interest It is interesting that this species, introduced for grazing, has been found to produce prussic acid, thus becoming dangerous to livestock. This condition occurs only during dry summers and after the first frost. A worldwide plant, Johnson grass is native to India, Africa, and southern Europe, especially the Mediterranean area. It was brought to the United States about 1830 for cultivation, establishing a stronghold in the cotton belt. It has become wild, reproducing by roots and seeds. Found in vast regions of the country, it grows generally throughout Texas. Perennial.

Setaria italica   **FOXTAIL MILLET**

top, early stage. D.B.
middle, prime fuzzy foxtails. D.B.
bottom, past prime. D.B.
opposite, design. G.M.

Early Stage Foxtail millet is one of the outstanding foxtails since it produces a beautiful head during all stages, although several other foxtail species can also be classified as decorative naturals. *Setaria italica* has sometimes become a pest in agricultural areas and at times difficult for farmers to control. Early leaves appear similar to Johnson grass, having a whitish midrib. Typical in early growth are the leaf sheaths, overlapping on the stem and with folding pointed leaves. Stems are slender, though bearing a large head weighted with seeds. Immature foxtails, approximately 2" long, are cylindrical, as green as the leaves and heavily textured. The panicles during growth are dense; however, the plentiful bristles, often purple, create a transparency around the perimeter, doubling its size. Depending on rain, there can be both a spring crop and a fall crop. Late April through June; August through October.

Prime Stage Fully developed foxtail millet ranges 3"–6" in length, sometimes longer if fertilized. The fuzzy foxtails are soft and flexible, and during development they nod noticeably on culms that grow 3'–5'. During this stage dried millet supplies a fine foxtail that remains green for some time. Smaller foxtails can also be cut at earlier stages. Past prime, when leaves and stems have yellowed and many seeds have fallen, the millet with less body can still be secured in colors from golden to soft orange. The green foxtails can be successfully used in fresh designing and are durable and lasting. May through July; August through October.

Design Foxtail millet is shown with many seed heads to create volume and mass. A glass vase was selected to complement the golden color of 400 foxtails and to expose the tall stems. American lotus flowers are shown dried, in the same warm tones. This example illustrates an exception in drying a species past prime.

Notes of Interest A species closely related to foxtail millet is *Setaria viridis* (green bristle grass), which is common throughout the cooler regions of the United States. Foxtail millet is distinctly larger and coarser. The Latin word for bristle is *seta*, hence the generic name, *Setaria*. As early as 2700 B.C., foxtail millet was cultivated in China. It was subsequently introduced into Europe and brought to the United States in 1849 as a forage crop. Other common names are germanica, Italian millet, and Bengal grass. This species is found in the agricultural sections throughout most of Texas. Annual.

Avena fatua
A. f. var. *sativa*

WILD OAT
COMMON OAT

top, early common oats. D.B.
bottom, pendulous spikelets. G.M.
opposite, design. G.M.

Early Stage Wild and common oats are easily recognized and are similar; however, each has different characteristics. Common oats, having escaped cultivation, are seen frequently in the locality of winter oat crops, showing growth at the same time. Wild oats are infrequently scattered and are slower in early growth. New shoots on both are abundantly leafy. These robust grasses are bluish green in color, unlike most of the grassy greens of other spring grasses. One to 2 spikelets first appear on erect stems, projecting from the sheath at the top leaf. Common oats: February through April; wild oats: March through April.

Prime Stage During this stage, the inflorescence of wild oats develops with 8–30 whitish spikelets, arranged as a loose panicle. These pendulous spikelets consist of 2–4 florets with long awns that grow as a continuation, doubling the length. The typical long and dark awns of wild oats contrast with the less graceful short awns of common oats. The spikelet of common oats nods with maturity on succulent, smooth culms. Both are similar in reaching 2′–4′ in height. A distinctive characteristic of wild oats is the attached spikelets, kinked and twisted on pedicels, appearing as if strung on fine green wires. Both oats are available in another color when left to dry on the stalks, losing many of the seeds from the spikelets. In this mature stage, and in this case past prime is an exception, the hulls are firm, providing a golden color instead of the soft greens. Starting earlier in spring, the duration of growth of common oats is longer than that of wild oats. Common oats: March through June; wild oats: April through May.

Design Wild oats supply beautiful decorative inflorescences and surpass in beauty cultivated oats when used as design material. Their beauty is enhanced by the flowers on fine stems and the threadlike thickness of the awns. In this design, two colors are shown, each from different stages. Also illustrated are the seed heads dried by two different methods, standing and hanging, for spikelets pointed upward and drooped downward. Both wild and common oats are beautifully displayed together with tamarisk and immature magnolia pods in a ceramic and wicker vase. Design by Anna Schindler of Columbus, Texas.

Notes of Interest Wild oats can be a serious problem to cereal crops by ripening earlier and dropping unwanted seeds. *Avena fatua* is a grass naturalized from Europe and at present is found throughout most of the United States, except the southeastern region. In Texas it is generally distributed in the Gulf Prairies and Marshes, Post Oak Savannah, Edwards Plateau, Rolling Plains, and High Plains. The common oat is a species sometimes found in profusion bordering fields under cultivation. As a crop plant, it too was introduced from Europe and now exists under cultivation and in the wild. Common oats are found occasionally throughout Texas. Annual.

Aristida purpurea **PURPLE THREE-AWN**

top, early stage. D.B.
bottom, prior to prime. D.B.
opposite, design. G.M.

Early Stage A true Texas grass, purple three-awn has innate excellent drought-resisting qualities. This native is decoratively appealing, having fine color and feathery seed heads. Early leaves of this grass, growing in small tufted clumps, are sage green in color. Blades are narrow, inrolled, and arched and extend 5″–6″, with some basal flat leaves. Culms grow erect, with the panicles developing fine awns, which are a subdued purple color. Although this bunchgrass emulates strength, it is, at the same time, delicate. Spring months and fall.

Prime Stage The slender wiry culms grow 1′–2½′ in height, and leaves from the basal clusters vary in density. Panicles are closely or loosely flowered, yet are not dense. The seed heads are narrow, and because of the weight of developed grain the spikelets nod. Prior to prime development, the purple intensifies and a silky appearance is created by the long wispy needlelike awns. The inflorescence opens on a main axis, with many flowering three-awned spikelets. The beauty of this grass is its fine awns, 1″–2″ long, which spread widely in three directions, creating a feathery appearance. When past prime, the wispy heads become open and the purple color wanes. Late spring through fall.

Design This dried design contains natural purple three-awn grass, flowers of Leavenworth eryngo, magnolia leaves, and cultivated gomphrena. In an ingenious technique, the inflorescences of the grass have been gathered together and held by a ring of bachelor buttons. The seed heads on shorter stems fall, displaying the feathery texture. The form of the magnolia leaves is repeated in the motif of the bowl. Purplish tones prevail in this design, ranging from the intense purple of the thistle pods to the soft purple tints of the grass, all complemented by the pinkish purple bowl. The use of natural materials with exceptional textures and color results in a beautiful creation. Design by James Kana of San Antonio, Texas.

Notes of Interest Purple three-awn can be observed growing in sandy locales along the sides of roads generally throughout Texas, rarely in the eastern parts of the Pineywoods, Gulf Prairies and Marshes, and Post Oak Savannah areas. Curiously, ants often colonize in the center of solid stands, obliterating the stems and leaving a distinct fringe of purple around the mound. This highly variable species grows well in loam and rocky soils, both in shade and sun; sometimes, with rains, it flowers most of the year. It is distributed also in Arkansas, Kansas, and some regions of Arizona, Utah, and New Mexico. The genus *Aristida*, which includes some two hundred species, is found throughout the world. In Africa it is particularly handsome, being a large extremely feathery grass. Perennial.

Schizachyrium scoparium   LITTLE BLUESTEM

top, early clumps. D.B.
bottom, prior to prime. D.B.
opposite, design. G.M.

Early Stage One of many bluestems, little bluestem is recognized as an important grassland species. It is also outstanding as a decorative natural. Warm days are needed for beginning growth. In early development it has bluish green basal shoots. Short leaf blades, 6″–10″ long, are extremely narrow, measuring ⅛″–¼″ wide; they sometimes fold. The fibrous root system is exceptionally well developed, reaching 5′–8′ in depth. The grass can be easily identified growing in clumps, casting a distinct muted blue haze. During development, before seed heads mature and color changes, the many pointed stems, neatly bunched into the clump, appear at various levels. Clumps usually measure 6″–10″ across. Spring.

Prime Stage Little bluestem slowly matures all summer. Stems develop with purple intermingled with blue-green, alternating throughout the height of 2′–4′ with a distinct delineation of color. Purple forming at the node line and vignetting upward into the soft blue-greens creates a beautiful stem, unlike most grasses, which remains colorful until past prime. Flowers develop as racemes are borne on a zigzag rachis. The spikelets are white and bear twisted awns, dainty and graceful. Both flowering and nonflowering stages are decorative. In drying little bluestem, the flowers are held securely attached to the stems by collecting when the inflorescence has just started to turn white, prior to prime, and the stems are purple and blue-green. Prior to this stage of development, without seed heads, the stems are an exception in use for fresh designing. This drought-resistant grass is lasting when cut green. Past prime, after a frost when the flowers have fallen, the stems and leaves turn an attractive orange color typical of some bluestems and remain strawlike into winter. Midsummer through fall.

Design The little bluestem design expresses a knowledge of its growth. The grass heads and stems are arranged separately to display their beauty. The jewel-like white flowers are significantly placed to achieve height and vertical line. Radiating lines are stressed by using only the stems. This design is a study in color harmony, using the soft greens of early foxtail millet, timothy, wild carrot, and mullein leaves, which create volume. The brown tones of magnolia leaves, fungus, and fabricated ram's horns display an accent in a darker value. Design by Mark Ruisinger of Houston, Texas.

Notes of Interest This grass was at one time the most abundant perennial in the central regions of America. It is one of the four outstanding forage grasses in the tallgrass prairie regions of North America. The other three species, big bluestem, Indian grass, and switch grass, are also decorative naturals. Due to its nutritious value, during pioneer days cattle were shipped to the greener little bluestem ranges in Kansas and Oklahoma for fattening. Little bluestem is native to all states except Nevada, Washington, Oregon, and California and is found essentially throughout Texas, although rarely in the Pineywoods. Perennial.

Chasmanthium latifolium **BROADLEAF UNIOLA**

top, early stage. D.B.
bottom, fish-scale pattern. D.B.
opposite, design. G.M.

Early Stage Uniola is an outstanding grass with a beautiful decorative inflorescence. During early development, this species is rich with leaves throughout four-fifths of the culm. The smooth stem, usually growing 2½′–3½′ in height, is unbranched with one seed head. Attractive flat leaves, wider in the middle than at either end, extend 6″–8″ long to a point. With adequate moisture during the cool season, this grass always appears robust. The freshness attracts attention to the true green leaves, which point upward. When leaves are almost completely developed, the inflorescence appears on the upper fifth of the culm as tiny yellow-green spikelets. Dotlike on long pedicles, they remain erect until the head is partially developed. Early spring.

Prime Stage A decisive marking appears as a fish-scale pattern on the spikelets. At this stage the spikelets, ½″ long, are compact and pointed at both ends. Strongly drooping with maturity, open panicles fall gracefully to one side within the curve of the stem. The flat, awnless, 1″ spikelets contain 8 to 12 flowers; with age, they noticeably broaden, losing the early, tight pointed form. At this prime stage, the color is bluish green. The spikelets will dry a celadon gray color. When used as fresh growth, uniola is also beautiful in the early stage. The luxurious foliage is then more important than the inflorescence. This cool-season species is available during spring and fall, yet becomes semidormant during summer. Mid April through mid June; September through October.

Design As a decorative natural, uniola is excellent for both dry and fresh designing. The natural curve of this grass is its beautiful feature. The graceful contour lines are emphasized by full seeds folding downward. The seed heads display textured patterns created by the spikelets. Combined with the uniola are old-man's-beard white pods of the male and female and one stem of splitbeard bluestem. The beautiful lines determined by nature give quality to this natural in its original form.

Notes of Interest Seaoats, *Uniola paniculata,* is another uniola species and is more commonly known as a decorative dried material. It is found along coastal areas and is a protected species, since it supplies bird forage. Inland seaoats, a common name for broadleaf uniola, is often found in colonies, growing in moist areas of shaded streambanks and woodlands. It is found, particularly in forested areas, in eleven southern states. Native to Texas, it grows throughout, rarely in the High Plains, extreme southern and western portions of the South Texas Plains, and the Trans-Pecos areas. Perennial.

Setaria scheelei   SOUTHWEST BRISTLE GRASS

top, early stage. D.B.
bottom, prime bristled spikes. D.B.
opposite, design. G.M.

Early Stage Southwest bristle grass can be first detected growing in tufts in shaded areas. The clumps are dense with an abundance of flat dark green leaves. There is a tendency for the thin blades to nod, tips folding almost to the ground during the early stage. Hidden among the leaves, panicles are borne on spreading culms, with little evidence of its typical bristles. Late April through September.

Prime Stage The grass, in reaching approximately 2′ in height, develops the first panicle on a taller stem, then additional ones on secondary shoots. Usually, the first spike is a prime example, growing well above the leaves, 3′–4′ in height. Due to sprawling culms, the spearlike inflorescences on secondary shoots do not appear as prominently erect. The spikes taper from base to apex, with the axis visible throughout the entire length. As its name implies, this grass is adorned with a wealth of bristles, seen below the spikelets. The beauty of the flowering spike lies in the magnitude of bristles and seedy spikelets. Inflorescences appear fluffy yet stiff in erection, giving airy bodiness. A desirable natural, it dries easily. The herbage and inflorescences are durable for fresh designs. May through November.

Design The simplicity of this design reveals the beauty of southwest bristle grass. It is displayed alone to emphasize its purity. In the grass' natural form, the bristles and textured seeds are clearly defined in the dried panicles. Design by Robert Palmer of Austin, Texas.

Notes of Interest This species can be found growing isolated in a few clumps and abundantly in wooded areas near creeks and rivers, shaded ravines, and canyons. Livestock find it palatable. In Texas it is indigenous to most areas, usually less found in the Pineywoods, the Cross Timbers and Prairies, and the Post Oak Savannah and in northern parts of the Gulf Prairies and Marshes and the Blackland Prairies. Perennial.

Arundo donax   GIANT REED

top, early stage. D.B.
middle, prime stalks. D.B.
bottom, flower. D.B.
opposite, design. G.M.

Early Stage Under favorable climatic conditions, this gigantic grass can reach a height of 20′. Its rudimentary growth originates with a stout culm, visible with a centered leaf rolled to a point, similar to a cultivated canna lily, approximately 5″–10″ in height. During the growth pattern, rich green leaves appear, alternating on either side of the culm. When the previous year's stand is mowed, the vigorous root system consisting of knotty rhizomes develops, shooting forth all new growth. In contrast, when the prior growth remains, shoots are intermingled among old stalks, creating an unkempt appearance. Late winter through early spring.

Prime Stage As increasing height develops, the leaves can extend 2′ in length uniformly spaced on the main stalk. The leaf blade characteristically is glabrous, flat, elongated, and tapering to a point, accentuating the unusual length. The round culm becomes shiny and the rich green softens. Hollow spaces occur between leaf collars and are apparent in existing rings in lower sections of the stalk. The prime stage for decorative application of this grass is between the heights of 3′ and 7′. Branching may take place after cuts are made at different levels. Past prime, the intensity of color and freshness wanes when stalks harden and become woodlike under dry conditions; however, mowing will ensure fresh vegetation, supplying more than one yield throughout the growing season. Flowering clusters grow at the tip of a well-developed past-prime stalk, much above the last leaf. The inflorescence is seen in many-flowered panicles, dense with chaffy spikelets towering above the foliage with plumes waving in the wind. The prime stage of the flower is beset with silky awns, tinged with soft purple, prior to the stage when the seed heads become downy and color changes to silvery beige. Grass: early spring through fall; flower: midsummer through fall.

Design Although giant reed is considered common, and in some instances a pest, there is beauty in the form. The reed is excellent for providing height in a design. The clean, strong directional lines upward dry to a tint of green. The scale is adaptable for commercial design when material is required for impressively large containers. In the decorative example, the natural, measuring 5½′ in height, is appropriate in an antique Mexican basket. Shorter lengths are cut, eliminating the tapering height to expose the hollow stems that are similar to bamboo. When this vegetation is shaped by removing the leaves, it is classified as a redesigned natural. The purpose of cutting foliage is to achieve a pattern and to aid in handling. Clippers are required for cutting the thick and relatively hard stalks. When used in a fresh design, flowers complement the color, yellow-green or chartreuse, intensifying its outstanding appearance.

Notes of Interest An Old World variety composed of six species was introduced by the Highway Department in the 1930s for erosion control in ditches and culverts. However, this hardy drought-resistant plant vigorously spreads in colonies to railroad tracks and borders of cultivated fields. Other vernacular names are Georgia cane and giant cane. Giant reed thrives generally throughout Texas, rarely in the High Plains. Perennial.

Bromus japonicus **JAPANESE BROME**

above, early leaves and spikes. D.B.
opposite, design. G.M.

Early Stage This grass is one of the earliest to appear in the new year with its fresh, pure green hue. It is easily seen growing in patches along roadsides or in protected areas where there is no livestock. The culm, leaf blades, and sheath in the lower section appear whitish in color, due to shaggy soft hairs. Purple exists on the awns at this earliest stage. The stems grow solitary or in groups. Late winter through early spring.

Prime Stage The grass develops into slender, delicate stems obtaining a height of 12"–30", depending on the region. The typical characteristic of this grass is the long hairy spikelets. During maturity the inflorescences become full and drooping, creating a graceful line. The overall color, including stem, leaf, and flower, is soft pale green. Spring.

Design Within the genus *Bromus*, Japanese brome is one of the more decorative, graceful, and easily dried species. The natural delicate form is best dried by standing in order to obtain nodding spikelets, which become prominent in the design. The color softens to a classic celadon green. It is displayed alone here in an appropriate vase to illustrate simplicity, with a touch of broomweed fastened to the column.

Notes of Interest *Bromus* is comprised of approximately one hundred species, both annuals and perennials throughout the world. Also called Japanese chess, Japanese brome was introduced from Asia and grows scattered throughout Texas, found rarely in the Pineywoods. Annual.

Tridens flavus   PURPLETOP

top, early inflorescences. D.B.
bottom, *T. f.* var. *chapmanii* at prime. G.M.
opposite, design. G.M.

Early Stage Shoots and narrow leaves of purpletop grow in tight clumps of 6"–8" in diameter, appearing in the spring. As the grass develops, brilliant recurved green leaves grow abundantly about the base. A tuft of short stiff hairs on the sides of the leaf sheath at the collar section is easily identified. The top blade is extremely pointed and characteristically hangs perpendicular to the stem. With moisture the seed heads appear almost overnight, fresh lime green in color. Spring to late summer.

Prime Stage During maturity, the growth pattern develops rapidly and, in a matter of two to three days, the inflorescence gracefully curves and nods to one side. The seed head then loses its green appearance and delicately unfolds to purple. This hue is apparent midway through the spikelets, creating a two-tone coloration. Purpletop is an erect, tall, colorful grass reaching 5½'–6' in height. When the grass reaches this height, it is often found fallen, broken at a joint on the stem. The outstanding characteristic at prime is an oily sticky stem, appearing as if it were greased. A variety, *chapmanii,* also has decorative uses. Its inflorescence has stiffer panicle branches, creating an open seed head with longer spikelets. It is characteristically less silky in appearance and more erect in comparison. Summer through fall.

Design This purple grass is complementary to all colors and blends harmoniously with flowers. The green intermingles with the spikelets, giving a salt-and-pepper, green-and-purple texture. Both fresh and dried, it is widely versatile as a decorative material. The seed heads are typically silky. This design beautifully combines cultivated flowers of Nerine lilies, gerbera daisies, wild *Sarracenia alata,* and purpletop grass. Design by Rex Minyard of Austin, Texas.

Notes of Interest This species is native to Texas and found generally throughout the state, rarely in the South Texas Plains and the Trans-Pecos areas and more abundantly in the Pineywoods and the Post Oak Savannah. It may also be found in the eastern United States. After the frost the remains still stand during winter months and appear like Johnson grass in an overall pattern. The dark purple color of the Chapman purpletop is not easily detected growing under shade trees. Although it is known to be found more abundantly in the Pineywoods, it can also be found in the sandy and fertile soils in the southern parts of the Post Oak Savannah and Blackland Prairie. Perennial.

Sorghastrum nutans   INDIAN GRASS

top, early stage. G.M.
bottom, golden seed heads. G.M.
opposite, design. G.M.

Early Stage A golden native, the tall and slender Indian grass is perhaps the only decorative species with yellow-bronze seed heads. The typical erect growing habit is easily detected in the early stages, as leaves and culms develop distinctly blue-green. Long narrow leaf blades spread characteristically at 45° angles from the stem. The inflorescence first appears high on the seed stalks, displaying delicate pediceled spikelets of straw yellow color. Summer through fall.

Prime Stage Rain causes the growth to mature rapidly in height. Although this grass usually ranges 3′–4′ in height, under excellent conditions it may reach 6′. Fully developed leaf blades are 4″–12″ long. A prominent clawlike ligule, at the section where the leaf blade attaches to the sheath, makes for easy identification. At prime, the plumelike seed heads develop into a mixture of yellow and golden bronze approximately 6″–12″ in length. Paired spikelets consist of hairy awns, creating a soft, feathery appearance. Past prime, Indian grass may be observed still standing during winter months when its brilliancy transforms to a burnt orange color. This grass is best harvested at the prime stage or just prior to prime. Use of the standing position technique when drying achieves airy and fuller seed heads. Late August through October.

Design The plumage of the dominant Indian grass softens the solidity of the container. Colors of the chocolate Mexican thistle pods, ochre-yellow wild dill, sprigs of orange-brown coreopsis, and warm tones of the grass complement the slip glazes of this earthy, handsome ceramic. Indian grass can supply height and mass to both fresh and dry designs.

Notes of Interest Indian grass is considered one of the most important of the tallgrass species and comprises one of the "big four." (The other three are little bluestem, big bluestem, and switch grass.) The vigorous nature of this grass allows for its endurance in wide ranges of extreme weather conditions, and its aesthetic qualities in the field are increasing the popularity of this worthy grass. It is found throughout most of Texas, more predominantly in central and coastal areas, often growing along the road in patches like some of the bluestems. Perennial.

Andropogon ternarius   **SPLITBEARD BLUESTEM**

Early Stage A native grass, this bluestem is appropriately named splitbeard. The silvery white seed head is characteristically split into a pair, indicative of its name. Narrow leaves curving downward with lower leaf blades are exceedingly long, up to 24″ in length, while the upper leaves are short. The grass matures usually in compact bunches, 2″–6″ in diameter. Even at this early stage, as the inflorescence starts to project well above the top leaf, the development of the white spikelet pair is obvious. Late spring through summer.

Prime Stage Branching occurs on the upper two-thirds of slender culms, which grow 2′–4′ in height. These lateral offshoots, developing from nodes, are extremely thin and produce many more hairy spikelet pairs. The spectacular fluffy white seed heads mature well above the top leaf, approximately 2″ in length, and exist on colorful stems that alternate purple and blue-green, much like those of little bluestem. For drying purposes, splitbeard bluestem is another example of harvesting at both prime and prior to prime in order to secure the flowers, as compared to little bluestem requiring cutting prior to prime. Following dry periods in autumn, the seed heads may develop after a rain, surprisingly in one week and as late as the latter part of November, after the time when most fall grasses are past their prime. August through November.

Design The flowering seed heads afford not only beautiful downy white qualities but also unusual detailing of decorative shapes. The silvery white of this species can be elegantly used in Christmas decor. This splitbeard bluestem was designed to hang from the foyer chandelier at the Stafford Opera House in Columbus, Texas, creating a snowlike focal point. Surrounding the grass is a rattan vine wreath decorated with clusters of pine cones, sycamore pods frosted gold, and hot pink and red ribbons. This dried arrangement exemplifies the decorations utilizing white and purple grasses and flowers found in adjacent areas. Two pedestal displays repeat the use of the splitbeard and rattan vine with spikes of liatris, Leavenworth eryngo, purpletop grass, pine, and rattan vine berries. Table centerpieces repeat the purple colors in the use of the native hairy-awn muhly, a delicate feathery grass. Woven Japanese honeysuckle and ribbons integrate design components of a natural holly, agarita, with other materials.

Notes of Interest This warm-season grass may be considered not as desirable as little bluestem. Both grasses, however, are equally ornamental and decorative in supplying unusual white naturals. Unlike most grasses that have hollow stems, the bluestem consists of pithy culms. *Andropogon*, the generic name, derives from two Greek words, *aner* (*andr*), meaning man, and *pogon*, meaning beard. The splitbeard bluestem, or beard grass, grows well in a variety of soils, enabling growth to exist throughout one-fourth of the southeastern United States. During the late winter months, the seed stalks may be observed with remnants of the white spikes on the stems having turned tawny color. In Texas, splitbeard bluestem grows generally in the Pineywoods, Gulf Prairies and Marshes, Post Oak Savannah, Blackland Prairies, and Cross Timbers and Prairies. Perennial.

top, early splitbeard. G.M.
bottom, prior to prime. G.M.
opposite top left, table decoration. G.M.
opposite top middle, pedestal display. G.M.
opposite top right, detail. G.M.
opposite bottom, design. G.M.

pods

Rosa bracteata   **MACARTNEY ROSE**

top, wild roses. D.B.
bottom, rose hips. D.B.
opposite, design. G.M.

Early Stage The Macartney rose, a dense bush, is almost indestructible and grows in great mounds 10′–20′ high. Many protective, hooked thorns appear in pairs and help to make this species impenetrable. Considered an evergreen, the bush is almost dormant and has gray stems during winter. In spring, the bush is refreshed with new growth of tiny oval leaves that are shiny and dark green. Delicate flower buds, 1¼″ long, are velvety, soft green, and extremely pointed. Buds open, displaying a wild rose, 2″–3″ in diameter with 5 broad china-white petals. Stamens are wide spreading, creating a brilliant yellow circle in the center of the blossom. April through October.

Pod Stage After the petals have fallen, the numerous stamens continue to be attached to the hip, forming a beard. During development, the hip becomes fully round and the greenish color mellows to tan, followed by reddish tones. An embossed dot replaces the stamens as they detach at maturity. Five very pointed sepals decoratively top the hip, creating a starlike crest. Deepening to reddish mahogany, the hip develops firmly to a smooth surface, having lost the velvety texture, and becomes a decorative pod. This period is the prime stage for drying. The pods are like apples and can ferment, so good ventilation is required. Clipping the thorns aids in handling. Flowers appear sporadically during the spring, summer, and fall months, supplying rose hips in succession. May through November.

Design Both the shape and the metal of this small vase are in conformity with the Macartney rose. The round form of the decorative pod is repeated in the bulbous shape of the vase. The warm color of the rose pods blends harmoniously with the copper tones of the container. Maidenhair fern gracefully unites the natural material with the base.

Notes of Interest The Macartney rose is a native of China. It was introduced into the southern regions of the United States in 1893. Grown specifically for windbreakers in the Gulf Coast areas, it protected cattle on flat prairies. Other vernacular names are wild white rose and prairie rose. *Rosa* is a Latin name; in reference to the prominent bracts of the flowers, the species was designated *bracteata*. This prolific rose bush, having escaped cultivation, grows predominantly in the Gulf Prairies and Marshes, the Pineywoods, the Post Oak Savannah, and sections of the South Texas Plains and the Blackland Prairies. Perennial.

Ratibida columnaris   **MEXICAN HAT**

top, intricate leaves. D.B.
bottom, color variations. D.B.
opposite, design. G.M.

Early Stage This species, although common, features a leaf with a distinct and unique decorative structure. Leaves are intricately divided into many segments, creating a filigree pattern. As many as 5 to 13 segments to a blade are then again divided into this tracery. The finery of these leaves alone is deserving of attention, as are the flowers. The heads, borne singly at the tops of the ultimate branches, grow distinctly proportioned on the upper third of the stalk above the leaves. Early disk florets are whitish green growing on stems 1½′–3′ tall. March through November.

Pod Stage The disk, beginning as a hemispheric shape, develops to a final columnar cone, the color changing to gray-green. This color changes during maturity to golden brown, correlating with the development of the petals. The conical receptacles containing numerous disk florets are draped with as many as 4 to 10 ray florets in variations of colors. Solid yellow ray flowers are beautifully contrasted with others of solid reddish brown or maroonish brown and others that are yellow tipped, fringing the velvety browns. Past prime, when the petals are falling, the elongated disk returns to its lighter grayed color and commences to dry and harden on the stalk. During this period—while the stem is still green, the leaves fading or shriveled, and the conical disk firm—is the time for gathering. There are disks that remain partially brown at the base and less gray throughout that can also be decorative. Ideal disks for design are those that have matured with less exposure to humidity and rainfall. Although there are late flowers maturing during fall moisture, they seldom reach a perfect condition for gathering. Spring and summer conical disks can be used with more success, having had the opportunity to dry partially on the stems. May through November.

Design Mexican hat decorative pods are a natural in developing repetition, an element of good design. Cultivated bachelor buttons add to this repetition by introducing a new shape and color. Osage orange tree leaves lend variation of form. One devil's-claw is applied for interest. The basket, with rounded, scalloped edges, follows the continuity of repetition throughout this dry design. When cut fresh the foliage is beautiful, showing intricacy and durability.

Notes of Interest In East Texas, the Mexican hat, or thimbleflower, develops into a larger disk, giving the erect cone a considerably more elongated shape. This herbaceous, hardy plant is found blooming in profusion from Minnesota south to Tennessee and generally throughout Texas, adjacent areas of Mexico, and parts of Arizona. In addition, two other Mexican hats may be observed in Texas. *Ratibida peduncularis,* a taller 3′ annual with yellow rays and leaves growing closely about the base, is commonly found in coastal areas, but also found inland in the northern section of the South Texas Plains. *R. p.* var. *tagetes,* a shorter variety, rarely taller than 2′ with flowers predominately brownish purple, usually grows in the Rolling and High Plains and the Trans-Pecos areas. Perennial.

Allium canadense **WILD ONION**

top, bulbous bud. D.B.
bottom, flowering stalk. D.B.
opposite, design. G.M.

Early Stage This dainty plant is rooted from a small bulb. The grasslike leaves are inconspicuous compared to young capsules that develop upright on emerald green stems. There is a grooved line down the length of the long, 6″–18″ leaf. The beginning flower is a single bud, opaque green, matching the exact color of the stem. Mid March through early April.

Pod Stage Flowering buds progress quickly, the flowers often developing in a matter of one week. The elementary growth enlarges to a fully formed bulbous bud, showing the cluster encased in a whitish green tissue-paper-like cover. Patterned with veinlike vertical lines, matching the color of the stem, the buds terminate in an extreme point. Leafless stalks range in height from 8″ to 24″. Just prior to flowering is the best stage for this use of these long-lasting wild onions. Placed in water, the bud frequently unfolds, exposing bulblets, often with tails. This flower does not dry successfully using natural techniques. Mid March through mid May.

Design This lovely design is the essence of spring's freshness. It comprises fresh young wild onion buds and early cottonwood seeds. Both are delicately scaled to the proportions of a carved oriental vase 5″ tall and 6″ wide. Selected from two species, perfectly scaled seeds, shown in the design, belie the fascinating fact that one comes from a delicate flower and the other from a huge tree. The motif of tiny carved buds on the vase is continued in the pattern above with the repetition of a similar form by the use of onion buds. Unity exists in this charming design, as the contour line of the twig gracefully curves with hanging seeds directing focus to the flower pods. Design by Scott Jenkins of Austin, Texas.

Notes of Interest The wild onion belongs to the Lily Family and is edible. It supplied the main source of food for Marquette and his expedition during their journey from Green Bay to Chicago in 1674. This plant has been prescribed for colds, pneumonia, and bee stings. In Texas, *Allium canadense* is found predominately in the Pineywoods, Post Oak Savannah, Blackland Prairies, Cross Timbers and Prairies, and the eastern half of the Edwards Plateau. *A. drummondii* is another common wild onion with shorter stems and leaves, generally found throughout the state. Perennial.

Nelumbo lutea   AMERICAN LOTUS

top, bowl-shaped leaves. D.Y.
middle, solitary blossom. D.Y.
bottom, lotus pod. D.Y.
opposite top, miniature lotus. G.M.
opposite bottom, design. G.M.

Early Stage In the quiet waters of Texas, the exotic American lotus, or duck acorn or yellow lotus, thrives to display magnificent splendor. Strong roots develop in spring, at least 2' deep in mud. Young leaves unroll and spread bowl shaped 1'–2' in diameter, supported in the middle by attached stout stalks. Circular leaves with depressed, or concave, centers float as a water shield or stand like a parasol well above the water. Winds catch the drooping edges folding over to expose a duller green side patterned with veins. The surface of the leaf is mat green, opaque, a texture unlike the shiny, china smoothness of its petals. Tiny, green sepal-like buds are borne stiffly pointing upward out of the stalk. Developing over the course of three days, the bud unfolds to a regal blossom. April through September.

Pod Stage Shading from pure white to pale yellow, the solitary flowers elegantly crown the stalk above the lotus leaves, lasting three to five days. Delicate petals and sepals grading into each other enhance the brilliant yellow receptacles, becoming less intense in color as they mature. Stamens equally as brilliant cluster around the base of the conical receptacles. The decorative pod is funnel shaped, flat topped, and deeply pitted with pockets embedded with seeds. As petals fall, the receptacle loses the yellow color, transforming to green, the stage for drying pods, which will be a slate gray-blue color. Brown pods are already dried, having opened their pockets and releasing the seeds from within. This aquatic herb, despite its unusual hardiness, stout stalks, and large leaves, is gracefully delicate. There is a continual succession of leaves, flowers, and pods. Leaves for drying should be selected from those that stand above the water. June through October.

Design The lotus design features the use of large leaves, pods, and blossoms as compared to the second display. The position of the leaves illutrates their natural growth above the water. Dried miniature pods, petite blossoms, and a small leaf compose the alternate design of 16" in height. The smallest pod measures 3/16" and the largest 1" in diameter. The leaf, used as a backdrop, has a 6" diameter exposing the pattern of radiating veins. Forms of all three growth stages are featured. Rice gracefully complements the delicate materials. Immature blossoms retain a pale yellow-green for some time. A 1930 glass vase coordinates the color and design of the lotus. Fresh green or yellow pods have beautiful form. Flowers are extremely fragile and are cut during an immature stage.

Notes of Interest Lotuses exist mostly in colonies. Although seeds and plants are widely distributed, they grow in comparatively isolated stations, except those that are under cultivation. They are found plentifully in the Pineywoods, Gulf Prairies and Marshes, Post Oak Savannah, Blackland Prairies, and Cross Timbers and Prairies areas and as far west as the Edwards Plateau. The tubers may be baked like sweet potatoes, new fresh leaves are processed like spinach, and immature seeds can be eaten cooked, roasted like nuts, or raw. Throughout one quarter of the world, the lotus functions as a decorative symbol and is held sacred. It is referred to frequently in poetry and prose. The royal water lily, *Victoria amazonia,* is the giant of the family. Queen Victoria, fascinated with its beauty, incorporated the veinlike pattern of the leaves into an architectural design in London's Crystal Palace, Great Exhibition of 1851. Perennial.

Rudbeckia hirta   BLACK-EYED SUSAN

top, immature disks. D.B.
bottom, flowers at prime. D.B.
opposite, design. G.M.

Early Stage *Rudbeckia hirta* is familiar to everyone and a native species with many varieties. Prevalent after spring rains, it is seen growing in large yellow patches, decorating the highways, prairie, and borders of fields and unexpectedly flourishing in some cultivated hay meadows. Early leaves, oblong-lanceolate, develop lightly toothed but rough and alternate on hairy stems. Flowering heads with immature petals, pale yellow, clasp weblike around the prominent greenish brown disk florets. April through August.

Pod Stage Leaves develop more broadly at the base of stems and become narrower and more delicate at the top. Plants grow 1′–3′ in height. Pure yellow or orange-yellow flowered heads, 2″–3″ in diameter, are borne on upper branches. The raised center, a disk, enlarges with variations of colors, ranging from velvety dark purple to chocolate to brown-black. It can appear somewhat flat across the top or develop in a conical shape to ¾″ in diameter at prime. However, the disk is not as highly pronounced as in the coneflower, a species easily confused with the Susan. The rays are either solid yellow or beautifully tinged with red-brown toward the basal portion. Just prior to prime is the stage to cut black-eyed Susans for drying. The colorful petals will remain and retain color. Either the standing or the hanging technique may be applied. Past prime, the flowers wane and petals droop and, shriveled, cling to the the disks for a period of time, depending on climatic conditions. After the petals have completely fallen, the disk becomes a beautiful decorative dried pod. Gathering Susans with petals just prior to prime supplies a colorful pod with relatively lasting qualities. Susans are hardy and last for several days when cut for fresh flowers. May through August.

Design A graceful design with subtle qualities is obtained in using black-eyed Susans, winter bent grass, and foxtails. Dark brown Susan pods radiate on both sides of the design, repeating the lines on the column of the vase and two round forms of the openings. Subtle colors of bent grass in variations of soft green to blonde were selected during early through prime stages. The grass supplies a flowing rhythm around the pods. This lovely dried arrangement is durable for one to three years. Design by Joe Wilson of Houston, Texas.

Notes of Interest The annual coneflower, *Rudbeckia amplexicaulis*, is easily confused with the black-eyed Susan. The distinct difference is that the coneflower has a higher conical disk and the leaves grow clasping around the smooth stems. There are thirty-five species in the American genus of *Rudbeckia*. *Hirta*, the specific name of the Susan, means covered with short, fine hairs. The genus name honors the Rudbecks, Swedish father and son botanists. This species had been known to appear first in the East through the planting of clover seeds. The Cherokee and Seminole Indians found varieties of *Rudbeckia* to contain medicinal ingredients for treating fever, headaches, and earaches. The black-eyed Susan is found throughout most of Texas and rarely in the extreme westerly arid areas of the Trans-Pecos and the Texas South Plains. Annual, biennial, and perennial.

Monarda citriodora   **HORSEMINT**

top, early growth. D.B.
bottom, floral clusters. D.B.
opposite, design. G.M.

Early Stage This Mint Family species is easily recognizable by the mint green leaves on square stems. Horsemint leaves grow opposite each other, gracefully bending downward, margins slightly toothed, the leaves lanceolate, growing to 4½" in length with blade points exaggerated by their narrowness. The early development of whitish mint bracts, above the leaf set, is as beautiful as the prime stage when the purple of the flowers is more prominent. During growth, the leaflike bracts that support the blossom seem almost a complete flower in themselves. Tapering to a tip, the bracts unfold in the shape of a rosette, exposing many spinelike bristles. Late April through May.

Pod Stage As flowers mature in whorls at the nodes, the arrangement of as many as 6 successive floral clusters on a stem becomes evident. In graduating sizes, purple terminal clusters create a tiered effect. Bristles within are purplish; the lavender petals are sometimes dotted with purple. The petals united form a two-lipped corolla resembling a dragon's head. The flower at its prime is velvety, and lavender is more prominent than mint green. Horsemint flowers can also be cut for drying, just prior to prime, and are best hung. There is a period past prime, after the petals fall, when velvety capsules with downy lavender bristles dry on the stem and the bracts dry as a lighter border fringe. These durable capsules on partially dried stalks appear as if pierced by the angular stems. May through June.

Design Horsemint in this example is combined with two other natural flowers and one natural grass. The container, a mottled early American pitcher, is appropriate for an old plant. Among the many decorative naturals are species that dry lavender, purple, and gray. As shown in the photograph, wild poppy pods are light gray, purpletop grass is a deeper purple hue, liatris is lavender-pink; all are in the same color spectrum, harmonious with the lavender-gray horsemint flowers. The pods are also displayed on branching stems to show the tiered effect. *Monarda punctata*, with yellow and purple flowers, is another horsemint species that will also dry as a decorative pod.

Notes of Interest The generic name, *Monarda*, honors a sixteenth-century Spanish physician, Nicolas Monardes, who was a writer on the subject of medicinal plants of the New World. Horsemint is an aromatic herb, often called purple or lemon horsemint. The lemon scent is subtle when fresh; dried, it has a pleasant aroma, with leaves and pods used in making potpourri and tea. In Haiti, perfume is manufactured from bergamot, another species of *Monarda*. This plant can be confused with the bergamot orange tree, which has also been used in perfumery by extracting the oil from the peels (according to *La parfumeur françois*, published in 1693 in Lyons). Horsemint is found usually throughout Texas in a wide range of soils. Annual; may be perennial in warmer climatic conditions.

Solanum elaeagnifolium   **SILVERLEAF NIGHTSHADE**

top, star-shaped flowers. D.B.
bottom, pendant berries. D.B.
opposite, design. G.M.

Early Stage Spreading from deep, creeping rootstocks, the silverleaf nightshade, or trompillo, vigorously grows in colonies, enhancing the roadsides and fields and brightening waste areas with color. A common herb, it blooms with heavenly violet-blue flowers that develop into interesting decorative fruits. On spiny stems, alternate leaves with wavy margins are covered with matted hairs, which contribute to the plant's silver appearance. Stems, usually solitary, grow 2'–3' in height, with foliage arranged along the branches much like the woolly croton. Wheel-shaped flowers, a few to a cluster, develop toward the end of branches. Five petals, united at the base to form the corolla, are centered with brilliant yellow anthers. The starrylike flowers, with upright open faces at prime, endure hot sun, continuing the late spring profusion of wild flowers. May through August.

Pod Stage Tiny pendant fruits develop from the potatolike blossoms. During this growth stage, the green color has markings that resemble wild buffalo gourds in a diminutive size. Green becomes bright yellow, repeating the colorful stamens, turning black past prime. The berries, usually ⅝" in diameter, remain in this perfect condition for several weeks, depending on climatic conditions. These bright berries can also be obtained green, prior to prime, which extends their decorative period in slowly changing their color to yellow. Summer through fall.

Design Yellow semidried berries of the silverleaf nightshade accent the walnut driftwood, some limestone, and an Indian gourd. Diminutive berries are dispersed throughout this decorative example. Also shown, to denote counterbalance of weight, are the larger, cherry-tomato-like fruits of the Carolina horsenettle. The gourd creates a note of interest and repetition of form. The yellow berries, often found among dried grasses in late fall, lend color to fresh Thanksgiving designs.

Notes of Interest The Solanaceae, the Nightshade Family, is paradoxical, belonging to the potato order, as do the Irish potato, eggplant, and tomato. Some species of this family contain druglike qualities. Interesting records of medicinal remedies of the ancient Assyrians include the Solanaceae. These species were also included among the drug plants used by Hippocrates. The horsenettle, *Solanum carolinense,* similar to the silverleaf nightshade, is a more robust plant and exceedingly spiny, usually with larger fruits. *S. elaeagnifolium* is found generally throughout most of Texas. Perennial.

Sapindus drummondii   WESTERN SOAPBERRY

top, flower clusters. D.B.
middle, green berries. D.B.
bottom, translucent berries. G.M.
opposite, design. G.M.

Early Stage The soapberry is a highly ornamental and fast-growing tree, reaching a maximum of 50′ in height with a trunk of 2′ in diameter. The primary stages of flowering, marked by white floral clusters followed by golden fall leaves and orange berries, make this tree one of the most desirable species for decorative use. During warming trends the creamy white panicles burst forth, extending 5″–10″ long and 5″–6″ wide. Their showy flowers intersperse the green hues during the freshness of spring. Past prime, the color wanes to pale yellow. Complementary yellow-green leaflets, as many as eleven pairs, 1½″–4″ long and ½″–¾″ wide, attach themselves to yellow-green branchlets. Leaves: March through April; flowers: April through June.

Pod Stage There are two distinct growth patterns in which the globular berries become decorative pods. As the tree is fully leafed, fleshy whitish green to lime green pods develop on slightly angled twigs. These are not easily visible at this time, because their soft green color blends into the foliage. When cut at this stage, the firm ½″ diameter berry is long lasting in a fresh design. The pinnate leaves that surround the cluster can be found extending up to 18″ long. Dryer climatic conditions cause the green berries to transform into a thick-coated translucent orange decorative pod showing the dark seed within. At this spectacular stage of color, the berries are most successfully used in dry arranging. With aging, the berries shrivel and with overdoses of humidity or rain the orange deteriorates to black. During the winter, after the leaves have fallen, the berries are often mistaken for chinaberries. July through winter months.

Design The photograph shows a decoration consisting of two flower species and two tree species. The orange translucency of the soapberry acts as a counterbalance to the solid brown black-eyed Susan. The choice of a basket correlates with the texture and colors of these natural materials. The sunflower is in contrast to the scale of the sycamore pods, creating an element of transition from large to small shapes in the design. The use of back lighting can dramatize the soapberry's color and distinct translucency.

Notes of Interest This tree has been cultivated since 1900 as an ornamental shade tree. Young volunteers grow densely in groups. The gray bark is heavily textured in grooves, scaling and flaking into chips. The yellow-tan wood is extremely hard and can be thinly split for basketry and framing packsaddles. Buttons and necklaces are made of the seeds as well. The generic name, *Sapindus,* has the Latin stem *sapo,* which means soap. The berries of the West Indies species have been used as a substitute for soap. This species was named after the botanist Thomas Drummond, who first collected the plant in the early 1800s. The fruit has been used for renal disorders, fever, and rheumatism. The western soapberry, also called Indian soap-plant, jaboncillo, and wild China tree, is found generally throughout Texas. In the higher elevations during winter, after the leaves have fallen, the berries may be observed dried in perfect form.

Ailanthus altissima — TREE OF HEAVEN

top, flowers. D.B.
middle, lemon samara clusters. D.B.
bottom, red-orange samara clusters. D.B.
opposite, design. G.M.

Early Stage The colorful tree of heaven is well named, for it sometimes reaches 100′ toward the sky. Buds and tiny leaves are red. Red pigment occurs from the early leaf through the final stage of the fruit. Early red leaves are replaced by a beautiful color combination of soft purple tips and rich green found on partially matured leaves. Unusually long, on approximately a 2′ axis, 11 to 14 leaflets develop in pairs, ending the pinnate leaf with a small, single leaflet. There is a noticeable distinction in the bark of smooth, dove gray young trees as compared to that of old trees of dark brownish gray with fissured texture. Loose clusters of tiny flowers appear on terminal, branched panicles, 6″–12″ long. Their form and color are similar to the western soapberry. These yellowish green flowers are short-lived and less impressive than the seed clusters that follow. Spring.

Pod Stage The fruit is a cluster of many winged seed samaras, much like that of the ash tree. The seed is embedded in the center of a thin, membranous samara that is twisted, enabling it to travel airborne for some distance. The clusters are showy, lemon-white, and develop into pinkish with cream at this desirable stage for drying. At their height of color, the deep red seed fruits can easily be seen against handsome leaves. Greatly affected by atmospheric conditions, the samaras turn russet and lose the intensity of color with maturity. The many seeds create a decorative fruit that provides texture and repetition. Spring through early summer.

Design Dried seed samaras of the tree of heaven are shown in a wooden vase. The branches display heart-shaped marks that are scars where the leaves have been removed. The clusters resemble dried hydrangeas in color and texture, and they dry similarly, blondish with subtle color tints.

Notes of Interest Also called copal and Chinese sumac, this tree is a native of China. Introduced to the United States as a cultivated ornamental, in Texas and elsewhere it has become a wild species. Like the sycamore tree, it thrives in unfavorable conditions and is resistant to smoke and dust. Extremely hardy, it rapidly expands by seed, suckers, and fast-growing seedlings. Oddly, it can be found cramped against buildings and in cracks of pavements. Much of its use has been in supplying resin, which is in turn used for incense. Because it will take a high polish, the tree of heaven wood is often used in making fishing boats and sometimes in making furniture. The flowers are polygamous. *Ailanthus,* the generic name, derives from *ailanto,* a Chinese name meaning "tree of heaven," referring to its height. The powdered bark has been used to treat abdominal complaints, dysentery, and tapeworms. The distribution in the United States is extensive. This decorative tree can be found growing in the eastern states as far north as Massachusetts and westward to the Pacific Coast. In arid parts of Arizona the tree thrives in the occasional oasis. The tree of heaven can be found growing more frequently in light soils of areas east of the Edwards Plateau and the Cross Timbers and Prairies.

Maclura pomifera   **BOIS D'ARC**

top, early bearded fruit. D.B.
bottom, horseapple. D.B.
opposite, design. G.M.

Early Stage Of the many fruit-bearing trees of Texas, perhaps the bois d'arc attracts more attention and comment than others of its kind for its interesting fruit. The flower, although obscure, develops into an astonishingly large and textured horseapple. At an early stage, the yellow-green flowers of the female fuse together to form a green cluster the size of a golf ball composed of many hard drupelets characteristically full of milky latex. When the branch is cut, white beads of this juice immediately appear on the surface of the fruit. The early fruit is curiously bearded with long hairs, oddly orange-tan, much like the color of its wood. The male flowers are in a yellowish linear cluster and are found on separate trees. Leaves are ovate-lanceolate 3″–6″ long and become exceedingly lustrous with growth. Prominent whitish veins are in contrast to the dark green on the under surface of the leaf. March through May.

Pod Stage The hairs disappear during development of the fruit, being replaced by a heavy texture and conspicuous color. The brilliancy of the lime green, on some trees pure chartreuse, is striking to the eye. The surface of the horseapple is rough and bumpy, resembling the texture of a navel orange. The pithy consistency of the fruit is rubbery and when the fruit is removed from the stem the sticky latex exudes. At this prime stage the indehiscent grapefruit-size ball becomes a decorative pod for fresh designing. Bois d'arc apples cannot be dried in their entirety; however, they have been sliced and baked, as well as assembled as dried flower pods. The leaves contain latex and during their prime are relatively pliable. May through November.

Design This stunning fresh design is composed of bois d'arc apples, coralvine, green foxtail millet, and rubrum lilies. The horseapples are designed as a mound in the carved wooden bowl to hold the fresh flowers and grasses. The combination of brilliant green and pink colors glamorizes this design. Fresh horseapples are attractive, too, on the limb when the leaves are eliminated. Design by James Browning of Houston, Texas.

Notes of Interest The bois d'arc tree, also called osage orange, is native to Texas and naturalized in other parts of the United States. This fast-growing tree has been cultivated since 1880. It was popular for hedgerows and windbreak throughout America until the time when barbed wire was introduced. The genus was named for William Maclure, founder of the Academy of Natural Sciences in Philadelphia and an early geologist. *Pomifera*, the specific name, means fruit bearing. Osage derives from the Osage River. The name also applied to a tribe of North American Indians that prized the wood for bows and war clubs. Bois d'arc derives from the French, meaning "bow-wood." The wood is yellow and yellow dye has been made from the root bark. The bark contains tannin and can be used for leather tanning. This species is distinguished also by its sharp thorns on leaf stalks and young growth. There is a thornless variety known as *Maclura pomifera* var. *inermis*. Bois d'arc trees are found generally from the Pineywoods, Gulf Prairies and Marshes, and Cross Timbers and Prairies west into sections of the Edwards Plateau and the Trans-Pecos.

Parkinsonia aculeata **RETAMA**

top, tree without leaf. G.M.
middle, early leaves and thorns. D.B.
bottom, flowers. D.B.
opposite, design. G.M.

Early Stage A persistent spiny plant with an extraordinary "will" to live, the retama, or paloverde, can be seen existing even in crevices of cement. Brilliant lime green branches sprout from the older brown trunks. Smaller limbs regain color when recovering from dormancy. Retama is one of the first shrublike trees to rejuvenate its gorgeous green. This greening occurs under favorable climatic conditions, sometimes in a period of one week. The retama is an ornamental with lacey and airy branches. The leaves are 12"–16" with many tiny leaflets in 25–30 pairs creating the plume effect. Thorns are prevalent, often orange, and large even on young trees. Late winter through early spring.

Pod Stage The retama is a colorful tree with vivid greens complemented by brilliant yellow flowers. Borne in clusters, the flowers are hidden among the foliage in early development, becoming showy during maturity. Early green legumes, the color of the leaves, are narrow, long, and delicately pointed at both ends. During growth the 2"–6" bean pod becomes noticeably constricted between the swollen seeds throughout its length. At prime the green becomes cocoa color; it darkens with maturity. Its intricate and airy foliage affords a pleasant effect with fresh flowers. The few larger thorns on lower limbs may easily be clipped. June through August.

Design The paloverde is shown as a dried example of its bean pods and foliage in a contemporary frosted cylinder. The distinct narrowness and divisions of the seeds offer a variety of a decorative pod in shape and size as compared to the bagpod and trumpet vine. Foliage for drying is best selected after many of the leaflets have dropped, leaving a graceful linear axis.

Notes of Interest John Parkinson was an English author of herbal literature of the seventeenth century. The generic name was given in his honor. *Aculeata,* the specific name, refers to its spines. The pods are nutritious and eaten by livestock, from which usage the vernacular name "horsebean" derives. The seeds were pulverized to make flour by Indians. The leaves have been used as a remedy for diabetes and epilepsy. Resistant to most insects and diseases, the retama has been desirably grown as ornamental hedges. Another common name is Jerusalem thorn. The retama is generally found in the southern parts of the Gulf Prairies and Marshes, Blackland Prairies, South Texas Plains, Edwards Plateau, and the Trans-Pecos. It can also be found westward in the dry warm areas of New Mexico and Arizona and south into Mexico and Central and South America.

Melia azedarach   CHINABERRY

top, flower buds. D.B.
middle, detail. D.B.
bottom, masses of drupelets. G.M.
opposite, design. G.M.

Early Stage From purple to golden yellow is the season's color spectrum of this showy tree with maximum height of 45′. Leaves and flower buds together form a rosette bursting with yellowish leaflet points, surrounding the deep purple of tiny blossoms. Growth develops more rapidly on younger trees, especially on volunteers. In the developing stages, every branch tip of the chinaberry becomes a spectacular profusion of purple lilaclike flowers nestled among dark green and shiny leaves. Intricate, alternate twice-compound leaves composed of numerous leaflets have long petioles up to 25″ in length. Embedded in leaves, the impressive flowers with striking dark purple pistils subdue to pale lavender while maturing, camouflaging the remains of last year's pulpy berries. When selected in a bud stage the small blossoms are durable in fresh designing. Clusters of past prime flowers wane to dusty lilac-white and commence the development of the decorative pods.

Pod Stage After the purple blossoms are gone, the emerald green fruit makes a dramatic color change. Early fruits are visually lost in the abundance of foliage. Tiny, spherical shapes ¼″ in diameter expand to ½″–¾″ when the yellow pigment appears. Upright and crowded branches with masses of drupelets create a density unlike the delicate and airy loose construction of earlier blossoms. The period when green chinaberries are pealike, before yellow is prominent, is the prime stage for drying. When the berry, at a later stage, is yellow-green, it can be dried to a golden color by means of intense heat and adequate ventilation. Past prime, when the berries' intensity of color is lost, the consistency of the fruit is then pulpy and unsuitable for fresh designing and drying. Berries are slow in drying and require ample heat. However, the hard seed aids in retaining the form for a durable natural. Clear color is the key for selection when used in fresh designing. Throughout the winter, past prime berries are particularly conspicuous in large clumps. Mid June through fall.

Design Bunched into a lacquered, papier-mâché box with open lid, the chinaberries demonstrate repetition of design. The motif of the box is repetitious of the size and shapes of the dried material within. The long stems of these berries make it simple to assemble into bunches. A touch of split-beard bluestem grass has been decoratively added to the box lid.

Notes of Interest The chinaberry is of the Mahogany Family; the generic name, *Melia,* is an old Greek name, and *azedarach* is a Persian word for "noble-tree." Introduced into the United States from Asia as an ornamental and at times considered a trash tree, the chinaberry, also called the pride-of-India, has again been recognized as a decorative shade tree. Another vernacular name is Indian lilac. Because of its rapid growth it frequently has been used in street planting. The fact that the tree escaped from cultivation to grow wild explains its presence in vacant city and suburban lots. This species has been useful in the making of insect repellent from the fruit pulp, rosaries from the hard seed, and cabinets from the wood. It was a source of alcohol during the American Civil War—it had been known that by tapping the tree a toddy could be made and that from the berries a medicinal bitter oil could be obtained. This prolific tree is distributed almost throughout Texas, north into Oklahoma and Arkansas, and east into Florida and North Carolina. Another variety is the *umbraculiformis,* known as the Texas umbrella chinaberry.

Populus deltoides   **EASTERN COTTONWOOD**

top, catkins. G.M.
bottom, cascading capsules. D.B.
opposite, design. G.M.

Early Stage A stately tree, usually reaching a height of 75′ and 4′–5′ in diameter, it is recognizable by its massive structure. The first signs of growth activity are marked by flowers borne in catkins appearing on naked branches before the development of leaves. These clusters, yellow with pollen, strangely resemble caterpillarlike catkins hanging slightly curved, attached to pearl gray twigs. Corresponding with this formation are chestnut brown resting buds surrounded by tightly packed layers of scale leaves existing at the tips of branches waiting for spring. February through spring.

Pod Stage The blossom develops into a conical-shaped capsule on an elongated axis 8″–12″ long. As the fruit ripens, the vivid acid green capsules measuring ¼″–⅓″ darken and the capsule filled with silky cottonlike seed hairs begins to burst. The time for collecting is prior to the capsules turning brownish black and before the cottonlike seeds are wind borne. The abundant pendulous capsules resembling beads cascade on streamers and gracefully hang at various levels. During this growth stage, responding to warmth, the buds burst and rapidly unfold luxuriant deltoid leaves. The expanding pale, scalloped, yellow-green heart-shaped leaves are conspicuously smooth on top surfaces. Primary veins are displayed on the paler bottom surfaces. The fluttering leaves that rustle in the wind are easily recognized from a distance by their massive spreading branches that form a rounded top. Early March through April.

Design The dried example displays seed necklaces draped from a contemporary pottery piece. The dark color tones accent the black abstract slip of the container. Seldom do naturals dry as shown, dark brown to black. Gray twigs harmoniously blend with the pottery glaze and interestingly divert the tiny scale of pods from the pronounced thickness of its support. Even though the cottonwood is massive, it is the small capsule, diminutive in size, that is the most interesting component of this tree for use in a design. In a fresh design, green cottonwood seeds will last one week. Immature seeds have a continued growth with interesting changes over a period of several days. A strange phenomenon can be observed when seed pods decrease in size, becoming even more delicate, and the green color strikingly darkens to black, however remaining beautiful without deteriorating.

Notes of Interest The eastern cottonwood belongs to the Willow Family, cultivated since 1750. In France, during this same year, a new group was developed, known as *Populus deltoides × canadensis*, when this species was hybridized with another species, the black poplar. The genus, *Populus*, refers to the ancient name given by Pliny. The specific name, *deltoides*, refers to its triangular leaves. A vernacular name, "necklace poplar," refers to the long strand of capsule fruits. Other common names are water poplar, southern cottonwood, and alamo. The soft properties allow the wood to be easily worked with tools and glueing, however unsuitable it is for building. Many of these trees with huge trunks are disappearing to the paper, plywood, and crating industries. Cottonwood adapts to the making of musical instruments, and some species, virtually without odor, are used in making food containers. An ornamental consisting of female and male on separate trees, it is particularly common throughout the eastern United States and east of the Rocky Mountains. It thrives throughout most of Texas in moist, rich soil along streams, waterways, and culverts.

Aesculus pavia   RED BUCKEYE

Early Stage This highly ornamental bush is among the first of the native shrubs to show signs of life during late winter. At the tips of gray branches, the resting red leaf bud is suggestive in color of the blossoms that follow. Awakned leaves are handsomely glossy, rich forest green, and beautifully constructed. The palm shape is comprised of five leaflets radiating from a long petiole with veins diagonally lined from finely toothed edges delineating nature's precision. Late February through March.

Pod Stage Ruby flowers that follow after the leaf development make this bush aesthetically spectacular. The brilliant corolla, of five petals with tubular calyx, displays yellow stamens. Blossoms predominately stand erect on an upward axis above the skirted foliage. A succession of color other than the flowers is seen within the development of the branches: a line of gray twigs gives rise to brilliant yellow-green branchlets, which are succeeded by the red stems that are identical in color to the attached blossoms. Blossoms and leaves, as shown in the photograph of the rattan vine design on page 81, can be fragile when cut fresh. Flowering buds and the well-developed foliage on gray twigs lead to more durability. Immature foliage on newly developed branchlets is perishable. The red buckeye flower develops into the pod, a chestnutlike leathery capsule 1"–2" in diameter, and is in three segments. Flowers: February through early April; pod: late spring through midsummer.

Design Dried buckeye pods, which appear almost artificial, are shown alone to exemplify simplicity. The handblown glass container of earthy tones coordinates base and material, rendering unity. Usually the larger capsules open while drying, displaying the nut within. These nuts are smooth and appear highly polished. Early pods of small diameter dry intact showing the texture of the capsule. This example illustrates the use of natural pods in achieving rhythmical repetition of form.

Notes of Interest In certain local areas the pod has been worn as a necklace as a remedy for arthritis and as a good luck piece. The powdered bark has been used in domestic medicine for ulcers and toothaches. Indians found the poison of crushed pods useful in stupefying fish, causing them to float to the surface. The generic name, *Aesculus*, derives from a name given to an old mast-bearing tree. The specific name, *pavia*, is in honor of Peter Paaw, dating from the 1600s. Some common names are scarlet buckeye and firecracker plant. This beautiful bush with outstanding shiny leaves and colorful flowers thrives best in rich soils, particularly in forest areas of filtered shade. Commonly found in bottomlands and ravines along streams, it is indigenous to the Pineywoods, Gulf Prairies and Marshes, and west to the Edwards Plateau.

top, early leaves. D.B.
middle, flower. D.B.
bottom, pod. D.B.
opposite, design. G.M.

Platanus occidentalis   AMERICAN SYCAMORE

top, early downy leaves. D.B.
bottom, seed balls. D.B.
opposite, design. G.M.

Early Stage The sycamore tree is usually 90′ in height and in some locations can reach 150′. It is spectacular in the winter and early spring, almost as if it had been white-washed. The scaling bark, in thin sheets of mottled moss green, peels off in the summer and fall, depending on climatic conditions. After shedding, the underlying white bark illuminates the branches and upper trunk. During the months when winter scapes are void of color, this is a remarkable sight. New downy leaves, 1″–2″ long, suddenly appear appropriately matching in color the subtlety of the tree trunk. While maturing, the alternate simple leaves are bright green on the upper surfaces and remain paler on the densely pubescent undersides. They are clearly marked and heavily veined on their broadly ovate 5-pointed blade that is often wider than long. March through May.

Pod Stage A hardy tree, the female sycamore also produces a hardy pod, which persists for months in spite of strong winds. The underdeveloped seed pod is a ball, covered with a brackish green overglaze of hairs with a brilliant green core. On peduncles that can grow 6″ long, the hairs of the conglomerate globose fruit are less noticeable, turning to a creamy tan pod and remaining hard usually into fall. The single ball of flowers on fruits has a diameter of 1″–2″. In the fall or during a dry summer, when the leaves fall, these pods are observed always hanging pendulously, with stems starting to fray to a thread from being battered in high winds. The sycamore pod is one of the easiest fruits to dry while green. It should be processed well before the surface starts to soften and disintegrate. Summer through early fall.

Design The feature in this original dried design demonstrates textures from the American sycamore tree. Pods, bark, and leaves from this species are unusually decorative. The interesting bark from the tree has been cleverly applied to the container. The compact form of the tree pods fills the base to create a cachepot. This design reveals a concept that components of an ornamental tree can lend to original designing. Design by Charles Thomas of Houston, Texas.

Notes of Interest Drought resistant and fast growing, the American sycamore is a long-lived tree that has been cultivated for over two centuries. Fossil records show that the genus existed during the time of the dinosaurs, 65 million years ago, and has remained largely unchanged since that time. Other vernacular names are American plane tree, buttonwood, and buttonball. This beautiful tree has great resistance to toxic fumes and is successfully grown for city landscaping. The seeds are extremely small, averaging 175,000 seeds per pound. It generally ranges throughout Texas. Larger trees are found primarily in the rich bottomland soils of streams and rivers in the eastern half of the state, particularly in the Pineywoods area.

Sabal minor   **DWARF PALMETTO**

Early Stage The dwarf palmetto is comprised primarily of large fanlike leaves on woody stems. Its classification as a tree is of interest since it is trunkless. Light green leaves arise from an underground rootstock without evidence of stems. The closed fan of new growth, 4"–8" wide, is erect with compact segments. Projecting above the foliage, on the upper one-third of a single stem, are the flowers. June through July.

Pod Stage During development, the palmetto spreads noticeably in width, with segments of the leaves cleaving at the apex. A leaf can develop 4' across, having many dissected narrow segments, creating the character of the fan. Concave stems are smooth and increase in height or remain close to the ground. The fruit matures into olive green pods, consisting of round berries ¼" in diameter. Past prime the berries turn black. The weight of the pods often causes the slender stem to bend gracefully in a curve. Leaves, which become dark green, and pods are both decorative in use for fresh and dry designing. The tendency of the leaves is to fold after a few days. Leaves can be selected at various width stages. Immature leaves are easiest to cut in shaping the fan form. The pointed tips of each segment are cut on an angle, decreasing the size of the leaf and securing it from folding, as does a fan. This cutting technique is redesigning a natural, as explained also in the use of the giant reed, or giant cane (p. 26). Flower: summer; leaf: winter, spring, and fall.

Design The palmetto is shown as an Art Deco motif achieved by cutting all twenty segments of this leaf. The example illustrates a selection from an early stage when growth is taller than wide. The berries are superimposed in the foreground. Palmettos can be pod-like when the leaf is cut small to scale. This effect is accomplished by cutting close to the stem and cutting much of the foliage away. Dark green leaves dry slowly over a period of two to three weeks, becoming lighter in color, and remain a celadon green for a long duration.

Notes of Interest The Palm Family, comprised of three thousand species, is nature's gift to tropical people. Primitive hair brushes have been made from palmettos by pounding the ends of stems. Due to the fact that it is trunkless, the palmetto has been given the specific name *minor*. The dwarf palmetto, or dwarf palm, grows best in wet areas of the state and is usually found in the Pineywoods, Gulf Prairies and Marshes, Post Oak Savannah, Blackland Prairies, and rarely westward.

top, early stage. D.B.
middle, fan-shaped leaf. D.B.
bottom, detail. D.B.
opposite, design. G.M.

Ipomoea sinuata   **ALAMO VINE**

top, morning-glory blossoms. D.B.
middle, fruits. D.B.
bottom, woodroses. D.B.
opposite top, wreath. D.Y.
opposite bottom, design. G.M.

Early Stage This distinctive leafy and flowering vine enjoys rapid growth. Spiraling and twisting around trees, telephone poles, and high fences, it can extend to 25′ in length. The intricately shaped, five-pointed leaves dominate the vine, which is dotted with pure white morning-glories accented with purple centers. The blossom develops into an oblong, porcelainlike fruit, 1½″ long. Summer through fall months.

Prime Stage The alamo vine exhibits a strange and beautiful transformation: as the fruit bursts open it takes the form of a fragile miniature woodrose. A succession from flower to fruit to rose pod occurs over the duration of six months preceding the onset of heavy frost. The brown paper-shell fruit is the final and most decorative of all stages. The cover of the rose pod is a tiny oval that encases four seeds. The seeds are oddly shaped and three sided, one side rounded and two flat, much like a quarter of an apple. Midsummer to late fall.

Design The fruit is an exceptional dried decorative pod, so delicately constructed and yet so long lasting. Careful handling is essential, due to its brittleness. To serve as flowing lines in design or to mold into a form, such as a wreath, it can take the place of commercially grown vines, both in fresh and dried uses. The alamo is a versatile vine offering two distinct forms for designing. The fruits from an early stage are tear-drop shapes on green vines for fresh designs. The dried flowerlike pods are secured on brown vines for dried arrangements. The hand-crafted basket and the alamo vines, in an unusual treatment, appear interwoven, resulting in a well-integrated natural design. Design by Linnie Harris of Austin, Texas.

Notes of Interest Alamo in Spanish means tree. The well-known sister woodroses 3″–5″ in diameter found in other parts of the world, especially Haiti and India, have the same oddly shaped seeds, but they are much larger. A member of the Morning-glory Family, the plant thrives in both higher elevations and low tropical regions. This herbaceous plant has been used in an almond-flavored drink. The vine is generally found in the southern parts of the Post Oak Savannah, Blackland Prairies, Edwards Plateau, and Cross Timbers and Prairies in Texas, as well as in Florida, the West Indies, Mexico, and South America. Perennial.

Clematis drummondii   OLD-MAN'S-BEARD

top, flowers. D.B.
middle, prime stage. D.B.
bottom, past prime. D.B.
opposite top, J. Bailey design. G.M.
opposite bottom, design. G.M.

Early Stage This species, a woody flowering vine growing to 9′ in height, is amazing and beautiful to observe. The petite flower without petals in early stages is in great contrast to later stages when white fluffy and fuzzy masses flow away in the fall wind. The beginning growth produces a tiny green, sphere-shaped bud unfolding to a ½″–¾″ wide blossom. The base of the flower ranges in color from pale pink-violet to pale yellow-green. The upper portion is creamy white with contrasting yellow stamens. Spring through early fall months.

Prime Stage The female flower matures to a fruit of greenish silky tendrils, 1½″–4″ long, fastened to an elliptical one-seeded cover. Later it transforms rapidly from silky tendrils to a fluffy coiling, plumose fruit. This period between the two stages is the preferred cutting time to secure tendrils to their iridescent ball. The transition stage from silky to fuzzy and fluffy texture occurs rapidly. The beauty of the clusters deteriorates past prime when masses of fluffy seed tails develop and white changes to gray. Midsummer through fall.

Design This fascinating feathery vine attracts attention. The beauty of its white softness is not frequently found in natural materials. The old-man's-beard's delicate essence and translucent character create volume and provide a striking contrast in a black glass vase. The second arrangement is a more complex dried design sensitively accented with green lotus leaves, twigs, cotton pods, and a sunflower. Design by James Bailey of Houston, Texas.

Notes of Interest Male and female flowers grow as separate plants. Although usually found thriving on fences and bushes, its natural growth can take the form of vines sprawling on the ground in undisturbed fields. *Clematis* is the Greek name for climbing vine. *Drummondii,* the specific name, is in honor of the botanist Thomas Drummond, an early botanical explorer in Texas. Some vernacular names are Texas virgin's bower, goat beard, love-in-the-mist, and barbas de chivato. *Clematis drummondii* is generally distributed throughout Texas, and rarely in the Pineywoods and the Gulf Prairies and Marshes areas, and extends into parts of Arizona and Mexico. Perennial.

75

Campsis radicans — COMMON TRUMPET CREEPER

top, flowers. D.B.
bottom, pods. G.M.
opposite, design. G.M.

Early Stage The trumpet creeper, or trumpet vine, is among the most colorful and impressive flowering natural vines. It is a prolific woody vine, vigorously creeping on the ground and climbing high with aerial, holdfast rootlets in trees, on fences, and on buildings. During the stage when leaves are absent, the blonde color is clearly visible in the bark and the interlaced network of spreading branches. New leaves on the trumpet creeper develop more slowly in spring than those of most other vines. Leaves are darker green with a sheen on upper surfaces; on lower surfaces, the lighter green is dull. Growing 4 to 6 pairs of leaflets, a single leaf terminates the 12″ axis. In the beginning formation the flowers are in clusters, usually 12 to 16 tiny bell-shaped calyxes developing color in a transition of green to orange. The calyx, sharply defined by 5 wedge-shaped points, develops cylindrically, opening to form the long tubular shape of the flower. Long branches, often shooting out into space and covered with leaves, are strong, supporting the weighty flowering clusters and pods borne at the ends. The funnel form of the flower is approximately 2½″ long, unfolding 5 petal lobes in deep red-orange. This color appears again in the form of vertical stripes inside the orange funnel-form corolla. This two-tone coloration of dark red-orange and light orange stripes creates a stunning effect not easily noticed from observing the outside of the flowers. The trumpet shape becomes obvious at the stage when the flower grows 3″–4″ long. Spring through fall.

Prime Stage Handsome lime green pods develop in the form of 6″ capsules. Diameters vary from ½″ to fuller pods 1″ in diameter at the center section. With smooth surfaces, the pod is ridged lengthwise at two edges, creating halves. The seeds within are arranged in systematic rows. Under dry climatic conditions, the maturing pods lose their intensity of green, subduing to green-brown. Seldom are there as many mature capsules in the clusters as flowers. Capsules are best for drying when partially green. Past prime, capsules split open in two halves, liberating the many broadly winged seeds. Due to the vine's strength in supporting the weight of pods, the trumpet creeper can be successfully used to create directional lines in fresh and dried designs. Summer through early fall.

Design Pods of the trumpet creeper, silhouetted in an elegant vase, show as an example of a flowering vine. Masses of these capsules establish the style. Rhythmic lines are created by the direction of the linear capsules, slightly curved, flowing gracefully into space. Beautiful gray-green and olive green colors have been achieved in drying, with these colors being repeated in the vase. The magnificent strong and rugged flowering vine produces a decorative natural with distinct design qualities.

Notes of Interest The common trumpet creeper has been frequently cultivated in the northern United States. A native, it is considered the most typical woody vine of the southern states. In Texas the distribution is generally throughout two-thirds of the state excluding the drier sections of the Edwards Plateau, Rolling Plains, High Plains, Trans-Pecos, and South Texas Plains. Ants, hummingbirds, and bees are attracted to the flowers. As an indication of the flower size, wearing a trumpet on all fingers is a children's game, the magical play of witches. Perennial.

Ampelopsis arborea   **PEPPER VINE**

top, early leaves. G.M.
middle, immature berries. D.B.
bottom, prime stage. D.B.
opposite, design. G.M.

Early Stage A member of the Grape Family, the pepper vine is by far more attractive than, but not as aggressive or plentiful as, the grapevine. There is a distinct difference between new, thinner growth and the development of several years' thickness of 1″–2″. Slender reddish brown vines are strong, capable of growing erectly to 4′–5′ high, without support, before climbing. Early leaves are glossy red, becoming green as the leaflets on the lateral axes develop in 1 to 3 pairs. They are intricate in design, prominently toothed on a 6″ central rachis. The abundance of leaves develops bushlike at the top of stems. The flowers at an early stage are erect clusters of tiny whitish green balls, the shape of the fleshy berries they produce. Spring.

Prime Stage Berries are colorful, changing from lime green to pink to purple before the final stage of shiny black. The bark of older growth is whitish gray. Often seen growing upright under trees, these thick stems reach directly from the ground to the trees' lower branches. At this stage, it appears as if older vines can obtain height without climbing the tree trunk. Leaves are absent on the thicker sections but are seen high in the tree tops intermingled with other leaves. Also called the turkey vine, the plant supplies a natural material that is obtainable during three growth stages. Thinner vines of reddish tones are adaptable to making wreaths of small dimensions. When the leaves are stripped, interesting curlicue tendrils that aid the vine in climbing are apparent. The black berries that develop in the summer and early fall are beautiful in fresh designing. Older, thicker stems, measuring 12′–20′ in length, can be used in coiling larger wreaths. The long vines can be difficult to pull by hand, since the tendrils are attached to the tree. Gathering the vines requires more than one person or a mechanical aid, such as a tractor. If winters are mild, the vine is obtainable throughout all seasons.

Design Long and thick lengths of turkey vine have been molded to create this 30″ wreath. The characteristic whitish gray color and unusual configuration make it unique, unlike any other vine usually used for fabricating natural wreaths. This wreath has been artistically designed with red chilis, cinnamon sticks, and ribbons. It is an excellent expression of aesthetics. Design by Kathryn Miller of Austin, Texas.

Notes of Interest *Ampelopsis,* the generic name, is Greek, meaning vinelike. *Arborea,* the specific name, pertains to the vine's character of climbing in the trees. The pepper vine requires adequate rainfall and is best adapted to the moist areas of Texas; however, it can be found as far west as sections of the Edwards Plateau. Perennial.

Berchemia scandens   **RATTAN VINE**

top, early vines. G.M.
bottom, blue-black berries. G.M.
opposite, design. G.M.

Early Stage An all-season growth, this natural is an excellent vine for decorative purpose. In winter, due to the absence of leaves, the skeleton of the rattan, or Alabama supplejack, is easily seen. A network of twisting stems climbing high into trees, engulfing small bushes and interweaving branches, can make this species a detriment to growth in its path. On clear winter days the sun magnifies the smooth and glossy bark of colors ranging from dark olive green to orange-gold to red mahogany. Parent growth is usually dull mat green and well hidden among the offshoots. The leaves develop rapidly, often within one week, quickly covering the vines with brilliant yellow-green masses, camouflaging the stems. The leaves are delicate, 1"–2½" elliptical in shape, with obvious veins above impressed from the midrib. Winter through late March.

Prime Stage Greener color and pliability are more characteristic of the distinctly strong and many-branched vines during warmer months and rainy falls. The flowers that occur in spring are inconspicuous greenish yellow clusters followed in the late summer and fall by striking blue-black berries on short branchlets. These astringent fruits are beautifully arranged in groups on twining stems that comprise this handsome vine. Although rattan can be cut in the winter, the long period of growth at prime is a more selective time for color and variety of line. This species can be compared with cultivated curly willow, consisting of graceful lines, subtle curves with good design conformation. March through December.

Design A mixture of fresh green-and-brown vines, dominantly shown in a clear container below the waterline, is a unique use of the rattan vine. The container for this design is filled with movement, bending and looping in all directions, exhibiting creativity of curvilinear lines. Typical of this natural, a twisted length is molded about the exterior of the base. Extending upward, the movement continues and ends by spreading into space, terminated by a few tiny green leaves. All other leaves of this vine have been removed by stripping to expose the beauty of its line and variations of color. Leaves and flowers of the red buckeye have been added to the design to lend brilliancy. This species is in context and harmony with an uncultivated vine. Rattan vine, once dried, is difficult to remold; however, it can be shaped while green and has the properties of becoming hard and retaining the molded form after drying. Design by Lyman Ratcliffe of Houston, Texas.

Notes of Interest Alabama supplejack is an interesting botanical name and may refer to its pliant qualities in wicker making and crafts. In the eighteenth century, the Dutch botanist Berthout van Berchem was honored when his name was given to this genus from Texas. Rattan vine is one of the few vines included in the Buckthorn Family, which consists mostly of shrubs and small trees. Oddly, a kin species is the common jujube tree, a native of Syria that bears yellow fruit. This vine thrives best in rich, moist areas of the Pineywoods, Gulf Prairies and Marshes, Post Oak Savannah, and Blackland Prairies. Perennial.

Lonicera japonica   **JAPANESE HONEYSUCKLE**

top, flowering vine. G.M.
bottom, detail. G.M.
opposite, design. G.M.

Early Stage The Japanese honeysuckle, having escaped from cultivation, is growing uncontrollably fast, suffocating in its path some of the more favorable native species. Nevertheless, this common vine is extremely adaptable for designs because it is obtainable during all growth stages. Green leaves are apparent into winter, and the new buds reappear during warming trends. Leaves are ovate to oblong, growing on short petioles in pairs and opposite each other at intervals throughout the vine. On new shoots, which are often purple, leaf margins can be lobed or toothed. The tubular flowering buds are beautifully and delicately borne in pairs from leafy bracts. The white or pink pigment is purest at the tip of the budding funnel-form flower, just prior to opening. Vines: late winter; flowers: early spring and summer.

Prime Stage Leaves develop 3″–4″ in length, deepening to true green and becoming pubescent, with smooth margins and pointed tips. Fragrant tubular blossoms flare open revealing 5 stamens and 2 lips, one characteristically larger than the other, having 4 lobes and the other one lobe. Flowers in a succession of colors reflecting growth patterns—white, pink, and the yellow of maturity—can be found on the same vine. Where this species cannot twine and climb, the vine shoots will grow trailing on the ground with the aid of additional sprouting roots 16″–20″ in length. These lengths are advantageous in molding to create designs. Japanese honeysuckle, at all stages, is a workable vine due to its pliability and fineness in diameters ⅛″–¼″ thick. Suppleness exists except during very dry seasons, when vines become brittle. Fruits are tiny black berries, ¼″ in diameter, ripening September through March. Vines: late winter through early winter.

Design The primitive cross has been created by twisting many lengths of the honeysuckle vine onto a frame constructed of small tree limbs. The dimensions of this cross are 18″ × 12″. The applied dried decoration consists of the dainty brown shore rush, pods of the basket flower, the trumpet vine, and rice. The fine diameter of this vine is especially helpful in making crosses, hearts, baskets, garlands, and linear abstract forms. Japanese honeysuckle also can be used to obtain graceful lines when added to fresh flowers. Design by Kathy Burris of Columbus, Texas.

Notes of Interest *Lonicera japonica* was introduced from Asia and at one time was a popular cultivated vine in the southern states. Today the vine has become a wild invader. The black berries are favorite seeds for as many as five species of birds. During feeding, the seeds are transported by the birds to new areas. This genus was given the name *Lonicera* in honor of Adam Lonitzer, a German herbalist in the sixteenth century. *Japonica* refers to its Asiatic origin. Southern, white, and Chinese honeysuckle are common vernacular names. In Texas it is found thriving along fence lines and borders of fields and climbing in trees. Japanese honeysuckle grows well in moist areas along streams, rivers, and ditches predominantly east of the Edwards Plateau. Perennial.

Cocculus carolinus **CAROLINA SNAILSEED**

Early Stage A slender green vine, the Carolina snailseed, climbing into bushes and trees and twining along fences, is seldom found sprawling on the ground. The leaves, which grow broadly ovate 2″–4″ across, lend to a symbolic heart shape. The lower surfaces of the leaves are paler than the dark green of the upper surfaces. During warm months the greenish white flowers are born diminutive in size, developing into compound clusters on an axis 1″–6″ long. The unobtrusive flowers develop apple green drupes, usually not exceeding 2″ wide. Summer months.

Prime Stage Depending on climatic conditions, the vine changes noticeably from its all green growth to a brilliant red-and-green stage. Surfaces of the berries are glossy, adding to the decorative quality. Often the berries grow more abundantly high on the main stem, perhaps where the sun is more penetrating. In collecting the berries, care is necessary in untwining the vines so as not to cut and injure the main stem. Late summer, fall, and early winter.

Design A green-and-red Christmas design demonstrates the use of selecting only two fresh natural materials: mountain cedar (Ashe juniper) and Carolina snailseed. The female species of the cedar, having blue-green berries, is draped about a wooden natural form known as a *flores de madera* (flowers in wood), obtained from a tropical area of Mexico. Long lengths of vines without leaves emphasize the cherry red berry clusters.

Notes of Interest The Carolina snailseed can be mistaken for a smilax vine. The distinction is that the snailseed is free of thorns and has leaves that are less coarse and leathery. The generic name, *Cocculus,* refers to the curled seeds, which are snail like. Due to its showy berries, lasting through two seasons in some areas, it has potential as an excellent ornamental to be cultivated. Other common names are red-berried moonseed and Carolina moonseed. In the United States it grows eastward from Texas to Florida and northward to some central states. In Texas, it thrives in fertile moist soils of the eastern half of the state and is found westward but rarely in the High Plains. Perennial.

top, heart-shaped leaves and green berries. G.M.
bottom, prime berries. G.M.
opposite, design. G.M.

weeds

Croton capitatus   **WOOLLY CROTON**

top, early stage. D.B.
bottom, bushlike weed. D.B.
opposite, design. G.M.

Early Stage Woolly croton is considered a summer weed. Springing forth where it may not be wanted, it is, however, endowed with characteristics useful in decorative natural designs. Also called hogwort, doveweed, and goatweed, this leafy plant in early stages attains 6″–12″ in height and is relatively nondescript. Woolly soft leaves, usually egg shaped, develop opposite each other on erect stems. Leaf color is pale green on top, grayish green on the underside. June through July.

Prime Stage Stems become stout during development, with extensive branching creating a bushlike weed that reaches a height of 3′–4′. Flowers are tiny, in terminal clusters, and surrounded by leafy bracts that are whitish. In headlike groups, the female flowers, downy white, grow crowded at the base of the male flower. This species appears to be primarily leaf. The densely hairy leaves grow alternating on long petioles during this stage, as in contrast to the early growth of opposite leaves. The leaf lengthens and develops a lanceolate-oblong shape. At this prime stage, the green color increasingly loses intensity, becoming grayish green with silver white on undersurfaces. July through August.

Design Woolly croton in this example is shown in a clear vase to intensify the value of dried foliage that is greenish white. Delicate seed pods are creamy. Classified as an herb, this species with many leaves lends to drying as an off-white filler. Leaves dry folded, exposing the underside surfaces and are relatively brittle; however, after arranging they are very lasting. When freshly cut, the stems ooze a yellow substance that dries quickly.

Notes of Interest The *Croton capitatus* seed pods especially attract doves. A native, it is found growing throughout two-thirds of the southeastern United States but not in Florida. In Texas, it exists with shallow taproots in dry sandy soils, particularly in overgrazed pastures. It is found predominantly in most areas and rarely in the western arid areas of the Trans-Pecos and the South Texas Plains. There are two varieties of croton that are similar in appearance: *C.c.* var. *albinoides* and *C.c.* var. *lindheimeri*. Annual.

Gutierrezia dracunculoides COMMON BROOMWEED

top, early stage. D.B.
bottom, prime plant. G.M.
opposite, design. G.M.

Early Stage A common species with a wide distribution in Texas, this weed is known to many people. The conspicuous masses of brilliant yellow beautifying many terrains catch the traveler's eye in the fall. Broomweed is an active warm-season forb and evident in a variety of soils. From a central taproot the stem starts to branch in the upper two-thirds portion of the plant. Chartreuse-colored leaves develop first along the main portion of the stem. Leaves are very narrow and ¾"–2" long. As the broomweed matures, leaves become progressively shorter. The plant grows 2'–4' in height with leaves and diminutive pale yellow buds predominantly, on a rounded crown. Late July through August.

Prime Stage With development the leaves become less chartreuse, turning a darker green. Flowers, which are like miniature sunflowers, open as wide as ⅝" and appear at the tips of fine branches. The weed appears usually as a mound, peppered with tiny yellow dots. Fading, yellowish leaves fall when the flowers are completely mature and past prime, exposing naked branches. This species is typically harvested at this time to avoid the nuisance of tiny leaves that shatter; however, the beautiful yellow color of the flowers is lost. Commercial harvesters then spray the flowers various hues. The alternative to this method is to hand harvest and hand dry the broomweed. This should be undertaken before or sometimes at prime under good climatic conditions to produce a natural filler with yellow coloring. Drying during three to four weeks, the leaves fall from the branches and with gentle thrashing are eliminated. August through early October.

Design A small 6" broomweed wreath has been constructed using many green leaves and smaller branches. In molding the form, the leaves are compressed to hold them in place and to keep them from shattering. These leaves were selected just before the flowers reached prime. The daintiness of the blossoms on tiny sprigs is in keeping with the scale of the wreath. Colored bows and ribbons are mixed with the flowers to complete the pattern. This pretty wreath features broomweed dried from two different stages. By Maggie Herbert of Spring, Texas.

Notes of Interest Early settlers used this native plant to make brooms. A prolific species, unpalatable to cattle, it is found generally throughout most of Texas and rarely in the Pineywoods and the South Texas Plains. It is particularly beautiful in the Rolling Plains and High Plains, the Edwards Plateau, and the western part of the Blackland Prairies. Ranchers consider this extremely vigorous, drought-resistant plant a pest. Annual.

Rumex crispus   CURLY DOCK

top, early stage. D.B.
middle, immature plant. D.B.
bottom, prime stage. D.B.
opposite, design. G.M.

Early Stage Crisp like Swiss chard, early dock leaves are prominent and spreading, easily identified in the earliest stages of this robust weed. Usually wrinkled, with wavy margins, these curly large (10″–15″ long) leaves are exceedingly interesting. A pronounced labyrinth of veins running in all directions creates a reticulate pattern on the under surfaces. Reflecting certain climatic conditions, leaves are mottled green and sometimes mauve colors, which are then again occasionally repeated in beautiful specimens of the inflorescences. New stems, growing singly or in groups, are weak and spindly compared to the more mature development when they become distinctly erect. Late winter through early spring.

Prime Stage Perishable underdeveloped heads appear shimmery and as the greenish sepals mature the heads become firm. Stems from basal leaves develop robustly with whorls of dense green clusters on many branches. The seed, found in the center of the calyx, is surrounded by three heart-shaped valves. The valves act as life buoys in time of torrential rain. Prime examples are stalks 3′ tall, full-bodied, and covered with green seeds that create a textured pattern. Prime is the point in the growth pattern to cut for either dry or fresh use. The plants often display a stunning mixture of green and mauve shades just prior to becoming brown. Drying slowly, green stalks will turn a soft brown that retains the essence of the vivid green. At immature stages the fresh plant has little tolerance for cutting and will wilt. In drying, loss of color and shattering of seeds will occur. Harvesting prior to prime or past prime (brown plants) is not recommended. April through mid May.

Design The beauty of this weed is in its texture and color. Beautiful flowers are dramatized by the richness of fresh dock. The cool chartreuse green is complementary to the warm color spectrum of flowers consisting of Tulip Kees Nelis, yellow matchless lilies, and forsythia. The rounded form of the tulips gives strength to the massed area and provides transitions of volume in the height of the curly dock. As shown in the design, flowers with fresh dock look impressive. Design by Clif Lotspeich of Austin, Texas.

Notes of Interest Leaves of this species, rich in vitamin A and protein, are known to have been eaten like spinach. In the manuscript "Old English Herbals" by a Miss Rohde, this herb was mentioned as being used for patients plagued by the "Water Elf Disease" and by nightmares. Naturalized from Europe, twelve species of dock generally grow in fertile lands throughout Texas rarely in arid areas. Although a rugged weed found in sandy and rich soils of fields and road shoulders, curly dock grows particularly well in moist areas where runoff water in ditches and drainage water are available. Perennial.

Sesbania vesicaria   **BAGPOD SESBANIA**

Early Stage The bagpod is often confused with a similar species, the Drummond rattlebox, more commonly called the coffee bean. The bagpod is not a true woody plant. It is herbaceous and reaches 6'–10' in height. The long leaves are soft to the touch. The dull green leaves are alternate, pinnately compound with 10 to 20 pairs of leaflets, and lack a terminal leaflet. Summer through fall.

Prime Stage Flowers of yellow, orange-red, and red seem too dainty for this tall, weedy legume. With summer rains, 4 to 8 flowers develop quickly on long pedicles, red-orange being more dominant at first. The corolla is bonnet shaped, a form that also exists in the coffee bean flower. The fruit of the bagpod, in having only 1 to 2 seeds, rarely 3, is distinctly different from the several seeds of the 4-sided coffee bean. Bagpod seeds are loosely fitted within thin white membrane pockets, making a rustling noise when shaken. The legume is typically inflated, bladdery, and almost translucent in its fresh, pure lemon green color. Prime legumes for drying are lemon green. Past prime legumes turn yellow and then ochre yellow. This species is one of the more difficult bean pods to dry, due to the thickness and bladdery substance, and requires good drying conditions. July through September.

Design Bunches containing 20 to 30 stems of pods fill the colorful hand-woven basket. Bagpods dry golden color. The mass of the golden tones is a counterbalance to the many vivid ribbons woven into the basket. The form of the rounded seed pod recurs in the same form of the container. The two seeds are clearly defined and a sharp point at one end contributes an interesting design within the pod itself. When pods are being collected each stem is attached to the leaf, necessitating removing the foliage. Fresh bagpods are attractive, primarily due to their beautiful color. If care is taken to keep them cool, they should last for three to four days without water.

Notes of Interest *Sesbania* is the Latinized version of the name Sesban. *Vesicaria,* the specific name, refers to the legumes being typically bladderlike. This plant can be found in Arkansas, Louisiana, and Oklahoma and in the coastal regions of Florida and the Carolinas. Preferring moist soil, it grows in Texas more abundantly in the damper areas east of the Edwards Plateau. It can be found in low, moist fields and ditches, on shores of lakes, and along banks of streams. This native species can be considered unplentiful when compared to the abundant growth of the coffee bean, which is unusually similar in appearance. Annual.

top, flower. G.M.
middle, plant with legumes. G.M.
bottom, bean pods. G.M.
opposite, design. G.M.

Typha angustifolia   **NARROWLEAF CATTAIL**

top, early foliage and spikes. D.B.
bottom, prime stalks. D.B.
opposite top, details. G.M.
opposite bottom, design. G.M.

Early Stage Throughout the growing season the tall cattails flourish under various climatic and water conditions. Having a strong root system with creeping rhizomes, this aquatic herb can multiply rapidly in wet areas. Commonly identified as a marginal plant, one that borders shorelines, the plant actually grows in water. Extending in new growth above the waterline is a stout stalk comprised of leaves, 5'–6' in height, sheathing at the base, and a single spike. The extremely narrow leaves, ½" across, are true green, slightly convex with pointed tips and usually fewer than 10 to a stalk. In spite of their slenderness, the leaves withstand strong winds; however, resistance causes slashed tips. Spring through fall.

Prime Stage The spike that bears the fruit grows from the center of the stalk. It is a lighter green and smoother than the leaves, tapering to ¼" in diameter at the pod section and ending with a pointed tip. During development the pod is encased in a whitish green, parchmentlike sheath. As the sheath uncoils, the early pinkish brown pod is exposed, becoming orange-brown. Spikes appear as if growing double pods, one above the other. The two cylinder formations are separated by a short space. The lower pistillate, the female section, is bristly, grows 6"–8" tall, and contains hundreds of seeds at maturity. The upper staminate, the male section, approximately the same size, is fleshy with olive green pollen, brightening to yellow. The diameter of the pod is at least double the diameter of the stem. The prime stage in obtaining cattails is just after the sheath has dropped from the pods. At this stage bristles are secure from bursting into fuzz. This stage is usually a 4–5-day period. Foliage and pods can be dried at this time. April through mid May.

Design As shown in this oriental design, cattail foliage and pods excel in color and form. This design is a unit of three components: two containers and one rock. The special technique in this design is in the use of various growth stages of the entire cattail plant. Leaves are designed erect and bent at sharp angles. Immature pods are displayed in greenish color. Prime pods are orange-brown. Pollen cylinders of the spikes have been clipped just above the pod and others, with pollen remaining intact, are displayed in yellow-green. The unusual formation of the wild onion pod is its bulblets with exaggerated tails. Shore rush has been inserted in a pocket of the rock and used throughout the design to supply a soft texture. The inward direction of the curvilinear bear grass and the curving tails of the wild onion consolidate the three units as a design. Wild poppies are extremely delicate and the stems were cut under water to make them more durable. Their delicate pods are flat topped, with a radiating line pattern. The brilliant color of the wild poppies is a highlight in this harmony of green hues. Design by Mieko Cooper of Austin, Texas.

Notes of Interest Young shoots of cattails are edible. The pods have been used in making mattresses and torches. The more common *T. latifolia* has large dark brown pods and broader thicker foliage than does *T. angustifolia*. These native species are found in various parts of the world. In the United States they grow abundantly along the Pacific Coast, throughout most of the eastern states, and in regions of the Southwest. In Texas both species are generally found throughout, especially along the coastal parts of the Gulf Prairies and Marshes, as well as bordering rice fields. Perennial.

HORSETAIL
Equisetum

top, early stage. D.B.
bottom, hollow erect stems. D.B.
opposite, design. G.M.

Early Stage A nonflowering plant, the horsetail often survives as an evergreen during mild winters in moist and sheltered areas. Rising from creeping rootstocks, early stems 12″ in height are yellowish green. The outstanding characteristic at all stages is that there are many joints with scales, united into tubular sheaths that take the place of leaves. Late winter through spring.

Prime Stage As the horsetail matures in height, 3′–4′, the joints are clearly marked as definite rings resembling bamboo. The evenly spaced joints create a vertical pattern, which may end in a terminal cone consisting of seeds. This plant is very erect; sometimes whorls of fine shoots appear about the joints, falling like horsetails, hence the name. This new growth, which also becomes evident when stems are broken or cut, has a fringelike aspect. At the prime stage it can be dried. The hollow stems that are ⅜″–⅝″ in diameter are quite brittle; the thicker stems are more durable. The dark green softens to a celadon color. Spring through fall.

Design Horsetail is straight and severe, and as used in this design it emphasizes diagonal lines in an unusual technique. The focal point is China shine narcissus, interestingly cradled by the fresh horsetail stems in a clear glass container, exposing clarity of line. The Equisetaceae Family has been popular in designing, appreciated for its remarkable growth and freshness. This decorative plant displayed in a naturalistic turtle vase achieves harmony of design, uniting the material with the container. Design by Katch Bacheller of Austin, Texas.

Notes of Interest Horsetail is one of the oldest plants known to humans. There is fossil evidence that similar plants existed in the form of a tree during the Devonian period, over 300 million years ago. Approximately twenty-five species of *Equisetum* are distributed throughout the world, but only four or five are common in the United States. In past history, this plant had been eaten as a vegetable in Europe and Asia. The Romans especially enjoyed the *Equisetum*. The young spore-bearing shoots were prepared like asparagus. Horsetail, also called scouring rush, prefers the moist sandy and loamy soils of river banks, wet ledges and meadows, and edges of gravel pits throughout most of Texas but is found growing more frequently in the Blackland Prairies and on the Edwards Plateau. Horsetail is not a weed but a rushlike plant. A native to Texas, it is unusual in being flowerless. Perennial.

Natural Techniques

SELECTING NATURALS

In the decorative use of plants, form, color, texture, and line comprise the design. For either dry or fresh materials, these principal elements are the prerequisites in selecting beautiful specimens. The natural characteristics of some grasses, pods, vines, and weeds provide these qualities. There are many plants to choose from that will prove to be durable, lend filler consistency and provide interest.

Principal Elements of Design

Form. Clusters of soapberries, the cylinder of the mullein, the strange looking devil's-claw with antenna head and prickly arms, the exotic passionflower, Macartney rose hips topped with starlike sepals, eastern gama grass for antlerlike flowers, greenbrier with fascinating root configuration, the bulblets of wild onion, the pineapple shape of Leavenworth eryngo, and the feathery streamers of old-man's-beard, are all natural forms. Some species differ very little in form from the time of early shoots to maturity. Giant reed and the horsetail are two that can be used at all stages during various growth heights.

Volume is an element of form. In the use of decorative materials, the principles of design can often be coordinated by a filler consisting of volume. This material serves to provide continuity between the components of the design. Many designs need adequate amounts of material that create repetition to achieve this effect. Grasses that are full headed with many seeds or spikelets and weeds of voluminous characteristics serve this purpose, such as Canada wild rye and broomweed.

Color. Plant color is very evident during spring, early summer, and fall. The following are among the few hues and tones that are prominent: soft golden colors of foxtails, Indian grass, and wild oats; chartreuse greens of bois d'arc apples, giant cane stalks, shoots of retama, and young broomweed leaves; earthy browns of Susan heads, woodrose pods, and shore rush; lime greens of early horsetail, lotus, and trumpet vine pods; celadon greens of bromus and bristle grass; greenish whites of winter grass, goatweed, and fall broom sedge; pure whites of tree and vine pods; soft green-and-purple mixtures of spring and fall Johnson grass, dock, and purpletop; heather purples of horsemint, three-awn, and dropseed; oranges of fall foxtail, water reeds, and soapberries; brilliant yellows of the nettle fruits and broomweed; reddish maroon browns of rose hips; creamy beiges of Chinese sumac seeds, sycamore pods, and summer Johnson grass; grays of Mexican hat disks; coal blacks of smut grass; and purple-blacks of pepper vine berries. During the drier months, however, there is less reflection of pigment in growth.

Texture. Varied textures are found in beautiful heads of grasses, pods of flowers and ornamental trees, berries and seed covers of vines, and many obtrusive weeds classified as pests. Imaginative textures of grasses display long hairy spikelets, silky and grainlike seed heads, soft and hard bristles, and interwoven needlelike awns. Pods are velvety, cork- and cottonlike, mottled, perforated, fuzzy-fluffy, or sometimes leathery, satiny, or rough.

Line. Natural vines supply pleasing contour and transition lines. The expression of line is found in the free-flowing honeysuckle, the delicate alamo dotted with white fruits, the graceful curvilinear rattan, the directional force of trumpet ending in a pointed pod, the tapering turkey vine accented with curlicues, and the spaghettilike orange dodder.

Collecting Techniques

The most important factor in selecting species for collection (dry and fresh) is knowledge of the growth patterns and stages of each plant. In order to emulate nature in a design, this basic principle must be kept in mind. Insight and awareness of growth patterns are developed by exercising one's power of vision. The growth stage is the key indication of the time to cut.

Awareness of climatic conditions is important for collecting. For best results in drying materials, plan to collect when the humidity is low, since climatic conditions are utilized as a natural technique. Early mornings and late evenings are not usually satisfactory times, because of higher moisture content in the air. At such times, most growth contains a greater percentage of moisture, and the drying period is prolonged when vegetation is exposed to excess dampness.

In observing growth, one watches grasses, pods, vines, and weeds develop through their natural stages from early and just prior to prime to prime and past prime. Early stage is the birth of the decorative specimen. Prime in this context means the best and most vigorous period of the species' form and color. In many cases, just prior to prime is the best time for collecting. In other cases prime is better. Past prime is usually the waning of the growth's original beauty, although the exception to this is when a species remains beautiful past prime. The time for harvesting depends on the proper growth stage of the plant for the intended design usage, as shown in the following example.

Early Stage. In February the red buckeye bush stands naked, not yet with leaf, displaying the beauty of a gray structural design. Showing the earliest growth stage with signs of spring, red, plump, pointed buds exist at the very tips of branches waiting for additional warmth to thrust forth. The buds become intricate compound leaves followed by brilliant red-and-yellow flowers.

Just Prior to Prime Stage. The name "little bluestem" indicates in decorative terminology that the "little" pertains to its flower and the "blue" to its colorful stem and leaf. As the growth matures, the vitality of color is a mixture of blue-greens and purples, displayed as serpentine sections throughout the height of the stem. This beauty of color occurs in the just prior to prime stage—best for cutting. Prime is the development of starlike white flowers, and in this case too mature.

Prime Stage. Dock, which begins as a weak, spindly column, an early spring weed, develops to a tall full-bodied growth with clusters of spinach green seeds throughout the stalk. The undeveloped shimmering and wilty seeds transform to a developed firm formation. At this prime stage, masses of nephrite-colored shieldlike seeds sometimes can take on another color. Mauve tones develop under certain climatic conditions, adding to the weed's decorative qualities. For fresh or dry use, capturing this growth pattern when green or mauve exists is an indication that it's time to cut.

Past Prime Stage. In the foxtail millet, green seed heads mature to past prime with a golden color. The density is lost when fallen seeds create a beautiful grass with an airy form.

PRESERVATION TECHNIQUES

If the various species have been given the correct natural treatment, they will appear as if still growing in the field. In this specialized area of growing, living flora, simplicity is an important factor in achieving the desired effect.

Process for Drying

The technique of drying plants without the use of preservatives conditions vegetation to remain in a natural state for a substantial period of time. While it is true that treatment by preservatives aids in pliability, the color changes that may ensue are unnatural, especially in grasses. The techniques described here create decoratives that are relatively new in the use of naturals. This natural process of drying decorative vegetation serves to retain as much as possible the color and configuration. Colors are subtle and blend harmoniously with their settings. Form is emphasized in its simplicity. Natural techniques condition species to appear close to their original form.

The natural technique is not a difficult process, but one based on common sense and a simple application of treatment. The elements involved are the use of heat, ventilation, and avoidance of high humidity and direct sunlight. For securing color, the basic factor in drying is to eliminate moisture as quickly as possible. Species dried quickly after harvesting are more beautiful in color and form. Awareness of daily temperatures and humidity conditions is necessary, for coordinating heat and circulation will activate the evaporation process to set the form and color. Experimenting with the requirements of each plant will result in the knowledge of the ideal conditions for drying.

Ventilation and absence of sunlight are factors that contribute to the drying process. A breeze furnishes natural ventilation and should be utilized whenever possible. Intense sunlight causes loss of natural color. The exposure of material to direct sunlight should be avoided from the time of harvest through its use in the finished design.

Areas. Attics and tightly enclosed metal buildings are excellent areas for drying. However, the condition of the materials should be periodically inspected, for brittleness and shattering will result with prolonged exposure to heat. The suggested time of three to four days is the tolerance span of exposure to over 100° temperature. Because ventilation aids the process, a cross current of air should be created.

Lines for hanging and containers for standing can be placed indoors or outdoors. The areas should provide protection from sun and dampness. Areas should be well ventilated by either breeze outdoors or air circulation indoors from open windows, a fan, or air conditioning. A useful technique in hanging bunches is to straddle the material on a line, allowing air to circulate through the center. Tangled and voluminous bunches may be difficult to divide. In this case, bend open a paper clip into two hooks and attach one to the line and the other to a rubber band around the bunch.

Methods: Hanging or Standing. The form desired is molded by the methods of hanging or standing. Either position will mold the form. Grasses in a hanging position will dry with heads and stems straight and pointed. The spikelets close inward parallel to the stem. The seed heads dried in an upright standing position become fuller, with spikelets taking on a downward direction. Seed heads may be molded to a curve or nod by placing the stems in a tilted standing position. Pods usually have shorter stems and can be dried by hanging or standing. In contrast to grasses, the form of most pods is not altered by the position in which they are dried.

Vines with attached pods—alamo, trumpet, and old-man's-beard—are best dried by hanging because of their bulk. However, such vines as rattan vine and pepper vine that are to be molded into a design should be cut during green growth for pliability and not selected during dormancy. Stripping, the removal of all leaves, is necessary. In this case, while vines are drying, the form is firmly molded by twisting, braiding, and weaving. If honeysuckle or young growth of pepper vine is to be used for this purpose, it can be soaked in water if drying is taking place too quickly. Soaking for a few hours to a few days will restore pliability. Rattan vine is an exception, for once dried its hard consistency is set. Soaking will cause pods on vines to deteriorate, and common sense indicates that this treatment should not be applied.

Weeds that are cut with shorter stems can be dried by hanging or standing. If long stems are desired, the hanging position is easier for drying. Such species as dock, when cut to achieve height, is extremely heavy and more successfully dried by hanging. The weight causes the material to be top-heavy. The same treatment is successful for cattail pods and foliage.

The size of bunches to be dried is determined by how small or large a volume one wishes to achieve. However, to make a manageable bunch, twelve to eighteen stems usually are best. Vines and tall voluminous species, for instance, dock, cattails, and giant reed, are exceptions. These bundles should contain not more than twelve stems. A system of bunching during gathering makes them easier to handle and transport.

Various sizes of rubber bands are more practical for bunching than string or tape. The slack is automatically taken up during drying, which keeps the stems from falling. The No. 33 band is useful for a large bundle of fresh or dried materials. The softness and width of the rubber will not injure the stems and foliage.

Containers for the standing position can be cardboard boxes of various sizes with or without partitions, wooden commercial fruit crates, plastic laundry baskets, or wooden bushel baskets. Wooden fruit crates allow air circulation between the slats. Cardboard boxes should be perforated on the sides. Other containers need to be porous or large enough to allow air circulation. Many stems are hollow; others, as an example, some bluestems, are pithy and may mold.

Testing. Many species may not be suitable for drying. Grasses and, particularly, some flowers containing heavy weight of moisture are not successfully dried naturally. A natural to be considered for use by the collector should be tested to determine if it will hold its form. Certain grasses shatter and part of the inflorescence falls from the stem. Further testing is necessary, since various species may disintegrate, lose all of their natural color, and become pulpy. The consistency and substance are lost in the form. Tests of small quantities of a natural should be made before gathering larger amounts or before planning to cultivate.

When using natural materials, one can expect a design to last a minimum of six months. The form of the vegetation is by far more lasting than its color, which can change according to the species. The color may not remain as constant as the form, which can last for a maximum of four years.

Methods for Fresh Naturals

The same awareness and knowledge of growth pattern pertaining to naturals to be dried are applied to the technique of using fresh material. Observation of growth from the early stage through prime is essential in order to capture the ultimate beauty.

Advisable times to cut are early morning and late afternoon when temperatures are lower. When cut, fresh naturals are sensitive to heat and the lack of moisture. The combination of high humidity and temperatures is an unfavorable condition for cutting. Ventilation is necessary if the material is transported. The same care should be applied to cut vegetation as would be given to fresh flowers.

In spite of all precautions taken, some plants are not hardy and wilt relatively soon when cut. An example is the castor-oil plant. Its stalks and pods are hardy, but soon the leaves droop and lose their form. If an unfamiliar species looks attractive, an experiment may be done by cutting a few stems for testing. Tests for color-retaining qualities, loose pollen, and seeds falling from the inflorescence should be made. As an example, excessive pollen occurs when eastern gama grass is cut at prime. For lasting qualities in a fresh design, most grasses should be harvested at just prior to prime. Grasses past prime are unsuitable, for their freshness is limited and their color is waning.

Flower pods after the bloom are interesting in their form and are usually long lasting. The criterion for cutting is that the pod is on a still-growing stem. This applies to all stages of growth. As an example, when the Macartney rose flower has depleted, the hip pod is at its most beautiful stage, yet at this time, when the bush may appear almost dormant, it is actually still growing. In contrast, the Mexican hat produces a delicate green disk during the early stage prior to the development of the flowering stage.

The limbs and twigs bearing the tree pods complement the overall pattern. Such fruit as soapberries and chinaberries grow in clusters, which can be cut on long graceful branches or clipped into shorter twigs. Stems of the chinaberries can be picked, one at a time, from the branchlets and condensed into a tightly packed bunch to create volume, a desired effect. Chinaberries for fresh use can be harvested at early, prime, and, in some cases, past prime when the fall color is yellow. Soapberries are equally beautiful when whitish green at the early stage or translucent orange at the prime stage.

Fresh vines without pods are successfully used at almost all stages. However, during the period when leaves occur, stripping is necessary. The vine can then be used as a directional line in design. Vines with pods, such as the alamo vine, develop a fruit and are successfully integrated into other materials. Two outstanding vines known for their magnificent fresh berries are rattan vine and pepper vine.

All cut materials like fresh water once a day. After being harvested, the material will retain freshness if the water is changed daily. When the temperature is high, naturals will hold their vitality if they are sprinkled or misted. Bleach in water has been recommended to retard algae, particularly in hot humid weather; however, naturals that thrive in unclean water, such as the cattail, may be badly affected by bleach. Some berries and pods, even though used for fresh designing, do not require water after being cut. The single fruit of bois d'arc, bunches of bagpods, and chinaberries are examples. To remain fresh for two to three days some fruits and pods must be kept cool. Soapberries at both their green and orange stages and buckeye pods on limbs will also remain fresh approximately a week without water. Such pods and berries are extremely durable.

Long, pointed blades of scissors aid in harvesting, particularly with fine-stemmed grasses. With practice, one may develop a rhythm allowing the tips of the scissors to bunch stems while cutting. A knife is preferred for cutting fresh flowers, for scissors pinch the stems, keeping the plants from taking water. Long-handled clippers assist one in reaching trees and stalks that stand in water. If vision is limited, the length is protection to the hands. A sickle is an excellent implement in cutting cattails and stout stalks, freeing one hand to catch. A bamboo pole equipped at the end with a pruner, including string, is a valuable tool. The pruner can be interchanged with a special hooked saw for thicker limbs.

Natural techniques for fresh and dried decorative vegetation serve to retain as much as possible the color and configuration of the species. Knowledge of growth stages and the effects of climatic conditions is obtained by constantly being in the field to observe, as does the farmer in watching over crops. Recording dates, time of day, weather, and the locations is required in learning organized gathering. Great pleasure and relaxing hours can be the reward, whether a field trip to public land to observe, an opportunity to collect on private domains, or a close-at-hand exploration of one's own property for a surprise plant.

A COLLECTING EXPEDITION

The weather report is for a clear day tomorrow. It is June twentieth. Due to the spring warmth and sun, the lotus pond is beautifully speckled with water lilies and pads and juncus reeds growing where the pond is deepest. Having observed the continual growth while scouting in Austin County, I conclude that the time has come for the first harvest of American lotus.

A quick call to the friendly landowner for permission starts the preparation for the next day's field trip. The farmer appreciates the gesture and we avoid being trespassers. He is agreeable, since after our previous trip there was little evidence of disturbance.

Gear is collected by referring to a checklist: angler's waders (or knee-high rubber boots), two to three plastic laundry baskets with straps or string handles, several cardboard boxes with partitions already perforated, two water buckets, a sturdy pole, scissors, rubber bands, two to three light-weight cloths the size of sheets, drinking water, and lunch. We are on our way by 7:30 A.M., earlier than expected. With the lack of heavy dew and the promise of a clear day, the sun within the hour will eliminate almost all moisture from the lotuses.

Arriving at this peaceful, untouched pond, nestled between gently rolling hills, we are afforded pleasurable surroundings for the morning's activities. There are no shade trees, which necessitates parking the car angled to provide an area protected from intense sun and catching the direction of the breeze. Time is of the essence, as we quickly prepare to wade into the water. A basket is adjusted to one's shoulder, leaving both hands free for pole in one and cutting scissors in the other.

Commonsense precaution is provided to legs and hips by the waders, and the pole is to alert any moccasins to move on. Encountering snakes is unusual at this time of day, for it is past feeding time and the increasing sun limits their activity. The spiders that enjoy the habitat of the blossoms may defend themselves with a nasty sting, so we inspect each pod.

Two persons are required to gather lotus, one to cut and one to make preparation for the natural drying process. The cutter is selecting the green pods in a variety of sizes with stem lengths as desired and gently placing them heads down in the basket, taking care no pods fall into the water. Twelve stems are bunched together with a rubber band. The use of rubber bands will keep the lotus properly in place for handling while drying. Once filled, the basket is passed on to the helper waiting with an empty replacement. Leaves standing above the water are selected in various sizes and also placed in baskets. The pleasant breezes will aid our technique in drying quickly. We hasten to place the decorative pads, before they curl, between layers of newspapers. Care is taken to pack loosely, allowing air circulation around the leaves.

Two-thirds of the pond's perimeter have been covered carefully to select for quality and to find the diminutive pods to be used as miniatures. We leave for the little creatures the pods that have been marked by the grasshoppers, raccoons, and spiders that find them choice edibles.

The sun is getting high and the cloths are needed as sun protectors over the pods. It is almost lunchtime, yet, if we hurry, a few fresh bunches of green reeds can be cut before temperatures rise. The water is at its cleanest at the deep end where the reeds grow. This is the ideal place for putting a few inches of water in our deep buckets. Although these reeds are tall and hearty, care must be taken not to bend the fragile pointed tips. The hollow stems warrant a slight tightening of the rubber bands.

We are satisfied with today's gathering. There will be other days to return, for lotuses continually bloom all summer and into the warm fall. As soon as the lotuses are unloaded, those to be dried with heads straight up are hung on lines under the shade trees. The other lotuses stay in boxes in the shade, catching the breeze. Their heads will gradually nod in drying. Leaves are turned and then shelved in a drying shed with open flaps. Larger pads with stout stems are hung on lines, allowing the leaf to fold in half, emphasizing the wavy margins. The reeds are misted and ready to be used indoors. There are still four hours of daylight left. The pods and leaves are drying quickly, assuring good color; however, the stems will need a few more days of this weather.

Cultivation and Conservation

CULTIVATING NATURALS

Gardening at home with Texas naturals has many advantages. The resulting growth can be used for dry and fresh designing. Colorful native and naturalized species can be used in home decoration, in landscaping, and in attracting birds. It is a pleasure to cut from one's own garden. Designing dry arrangements from a garden flourishing with natural plant life is delightful. A decorative design is a continuing reflection of a plant's beauty after it has been enjoyed as it grows. A selection grown in home areas enables one to observe growth stages of species close at hand. Cultivated flowers are beautifully complemented by decorative grasses. They also provide foliage and filler for a design.

At this time the cultivation of natural vegetation for environmental and beautification purposes is being emphasized. In Texas a variety of plant life has become valuable decorative and ornamental material. These naturals are also drought resistant and hardy, thus conserving water.

In a home, a principle of design is coordinating the interior with the exterior. Texas naturals can enhance the visual harmony by transferring color, texture, and line from out-of-doors to inside areas. In addition to creating beautiful surroundings, cultivated native and naturalized species supply a source of decorative materials for creative designs. With the abundance of plant life in Texas, a few of the more decorative species, in addition to some of those already described, are recommended here for comparatively easy growing by seed and transplants, depending on adaptability to the climatic and soil conditions. In cultivation of natural shrubs and trees, propagation is more successful when seeds have been obtained from the area in which they will be planted.

Flowers

Heads provide dried decorative pods or fresh flowers:

Common Name	Scientific Name	Annual/Perennial
basket flower	*Centaurea americana*	annual
black-eyed-Susan (brown-eyed Susan)	*Rudbeckia hirta &* *R. serotina*	perennial & annual
black Sampson	*Echinaccea angustifolin*	perennial
common sunflower	*Helianthus annuus*	annual
horsemint		
lemon horsemint	*Monarda citriodora*	annual
plains beebalm	*M. pectinata*	annual
purple horsemint	*M. citriodora*	annual
wild bergamot	*M. fistulosa*	perennial
yellow horsemint	*M. punctata*	annual
Leavenworth eryngo	*Eryngium leavenworthii*	perennial
Mexican thistle	*E. heterophyllum*	perennial
purple coneflower	*Echinacea sanguinea*	perennial
red poppy (corn poppy)	*Papaver rhoeas*	annual
yucca-leaf eryngo	*Eryngium yuccifolium*	perennial

Heads provide dried decorative spikes, sprays, or clusters or fresh flowers:

Common Name	Scientific Name	Annual/Perennial
bluebell (prairie gentian)	*Eustoma grandiflorum*	annual
Carolina larkspur	*Delphinium carolinianum*	perennial
coreopsis	*Coreopsis basalis*	annual
	C. grandiflora	biennial
	C. tinctoria	annual
goldenrod	*Solidago radula*	perennial
	S. altissima	perennial
great mullein (common mullein)	*Verbascum thapsus*	biennial
liatris (gay feather)	*Liatris elegans*	perennial
	L. punctata	perennial
western ironweed	*Vernonia baldwinii*	perennial
wild dill (prairie parsley)	*Polytaenia nuttallii*	annual & biennial
yarrow	*Achillea millefolium*	perennial

Grasses

Inflorescences provide decorative heads and filler for dried or fresh usage:

Common Name	Scientific Name	Annual/Perennial
bluestem		
broom sedge bluestem	*Andropogon virginicus*	perennial
bushy bluestem	*A. glomeratus*	perennial
little bluestem	*Schizachyrium scoparium*	perennial
splitbeard bluestem	*A. ternarius*	perennial
broadleaf uniola (inland seaoat)	*Chasmanthium latifolium*	perennial
Canada wild rye	*Elymus canadensis*	perennial
eastern gama grass	*Tripsacum dactyloides*	perennial
foxtail		
Carolina foxtail	*Alopecurus carolinianus*	annual
foxtail millet	*Setaria italica*	annual
green bristle grass	*S. viridis*	annual
hairy-awn muhly	*Muhlenbergia capillaris*	perennial
Indian grass	*Sorghastrum nutans*	perennial
Japanese brome	*Bromus japonicus*	annual
oat		
common oat	*Avena fatua* var. *sativa*	annual
wild oat	*A. fatua*	annual
perennial ryegrass	*Lolium perenne*	perennial
prairie wedgescale	*Sphenopholis obtusata*	annual
purpletop	*Tridens flavus*	perennial
southwest bristle grass	*Setaria scheelei*	perennial
Virginia wild rye	*Elymus virginicus*	perennial
weeping love grass	*Eragrostis curvula*	perennial
winter bent grass	*Agrostis hiemalis*	perennial

Weeds

Plants that provide dried or fresh decorative pods and filler:

Common Name	Scientific Name	Annual/Perennial
bagpod sesbania	*Sesbania vesicaria*	annual
broomweed	*Gutierrezia dracunculoides*	annual
broom snakeweed	*G. sarothrae*	perennial
curly dock	*Rumex crispus*	perennial
shore rush	*Juncus marginatus*	perennial
woolly croton (goatweed, doveweed)	*Croton capitatus*	annual

Foliage

Natural foliage for fresh flower designs; can be used also for dried arrangements:

Common Name	Scientific Name	Dried/Fresh	Annual/Perennial
agarita	*Berberis trifoliolata*	dried & fresh	perennial
American lotus	*Nelumbo lutea*	dried	perennial
dwarf palmetto	*Sabal minor*	dried & fresh	perennial
giant reed	*Arundo donax*	fresh	perennial
great mullein	*Verbascum thapsus*	dried & fresh	biennial
Mexican hat	*Ratibida columnaris*	fresh	perennial
narrowleaf cattail	*Typha angustifolia*	dried & fresh	perennial
wild indigo	*Baptisia sphaerocarpa*	dried	perennial
woolly croton	*Croton capitatus*	dried	annual

Wetland Plants

Perennial plants thrive in ponds, at the edges of streams and rivers, in low, wet areas, and in bogs; they are grown by rootstock, tubers, or shoots. These furnish decorative dry or fresh reeds, clusters, and pods:

Common Name	Scientific Name	Annual/Perennial
American lotus	*Nelumbo lutea*	perennial
common rush	*Juncus effusus*	perennial
great bulrush	*Scirpus validus*	perennial
horned beakrush	*Rhynchospora corniculata*	perennial
horsetail	*Equisetum hyemale* *E. laevigatum*	perennial
narrowleaf cattail	*Typha angustifolia*	perennial
rabbit-foot grass	*Polypogon monspeliensis*	annual
roundhead rush	*Juncus validus*	perennial
sarracenia (pitcher plant)	*Sarracenia alata*	perennial
sea lavender	*Limonium nashii*	perennial

    The sea lavender, growing in salt flats and along coastal marshes, has been collected for decorative drying material for years, so that it is almost a rare plant.

yellow nut sedge	*Cyperus esculentus*	perennial

Vines

Vines can be used for natural designs. Although vines characteristically climb, the following species will sprawl as ground cover, requiring less water than cultivated species.

Common Name	Scientific Name	Design	Description	Area
alamo vine	*Ipomoea sinuata*	fresh pod, dry pod	morning-glory flower, intricate foliage	sun & shade
balloon vine	*Cardiospermum halicacabum*	fresh pod, dry pod	puffy green pod	sun & semishade
honeysuckle	Stripped of flowers and leaves, the following varieties can be used for designs:			
coral	*Lonicera sempervirens*	vine & red berries	coral & yellow flowers	moist semishade
Japanese	*L. japonica*	vine & black berries	white, pink & yellow flowers	sun & shade
white	*L. albiflora*	vine & purple-black berries	white & yellow flowers	sun & semishade
old-man's-beard	*Clematis drummondii*	vine & dry pod	pink & yellow flowers, white fluffy pod	sun
passionflower	*Passiflora incarnata*	vine & fresh pod	purple flowers	sun & semishade
	P. caerulea	vine & fresh pod	attracts butterflies	sun & semishade

Grasses

Drought-resistant grasses are becoming important as ground cover. The following can also be used decoratively:

Little bluestem *(Schizachyrium scoparium)*.
This native perennial grows in bunches with a deep root system, sometimes 5'–8' in depth. Short bunches are attractive in supplying a blue-green coverage. Mowing should not be shorter than 6"–8". Little bluestem will multiply if left to mature to the flowering stage.

Perennial ryegrass *(Lolium perenne)*.
This weak perennial is adaptable to all vegetational areas in the state, except the South Texas Plains. A cool-weather species, this ryegrass can be grown for winter and spring coverage. The grassy green color among winter browns is pleasing. Ryegrass can be mowed or left standing to reseed.

Purple three-awn *(Aristida purpurea)*.
Flowering results in purple tufted mounds. Examples of this perennial growing naturally can be seen in some areas even during drought years along roadsides and in parks.

Bird Forage

Many decorative flowers, grasses, and ornamental shrubs attract birds. Cultivating some of the native and naturalized species that yield edible seeds and fruits not only adds to our environment but also is rewarding in enabling us to observe birds' activities close at home and providing decorative material:

The following natural vines supply plentiful berries: greenbrier, pepper vine, rattan vine, Japanese honeysuckle, white honeysuckle, and Carolina snailseed.

Ornamental trees that provide fall and winter food are sycamore, western soapberry, chinaberry, tree of heaven, live oak, and sawtooth oak. The eastern cottonwood provides food spring and summer.

Common Name	Scientific Name	Description	Annual/Perennial
agarita	*Berberis trifoliolata*	shrublike, red berries	perennial
American beauty-berry	*Callicarpa americana*	bushlike, purple berries	perennial
broadleaf uniola	*Chasmanthium latifolium*	grass	perennial
foxtail millet	*Setaria italica*	grass, seedy foxtail	annual
green bristle grass	*S. viridis*		
horsemint	*Monarda citriodora*	purple & pale lavender flowers	annual
passionflower	*Passiflora incarnata*	vine, purple flower	perennial
pokeberry	*Phytolacca americana*	bushy weed, dark purple berries	perennial
sumac			
prairie flame-leaf	*Rhus copallina* var. *lanceolata*	shrublike, red berries	perennial
smooth	*R. glabra*		
sunflower			
common	*Helianthus annuus*	yellow flowers	annual
Maximilian	*H. maximiliani*		perennial
Texas persimmon	*Diospyros texana*	shrublike, black fruit	perennial
trumpet creeper	*Campsis radicans*	vine, orange flowers	perennial
wild plum	*Prunus americana*	shrub, red fruit	perennial
woolly croton	*Croton capitatus*	bushy weed, seedy flowers	annual
yaupon holly	*Ilex vomitoria*	shrublike, red berries	perennial
yucca-leaf eryngo	*Eryngium yuccifolium*	cloverlike flower, cactus-like leaf	perennial

Natural Fences

Some of the more interesting and beautiful species are protected with an armor of thorns. These can be successfully grown for securing natural barriers. An additional function includes the decorative use of foliage and pods:

Agarita *(Bereberis trifoliolata)*.

Agarita is an attractive evergreen prickly bush. Hollylike leaves supply fresh and dry foliage.

Bois d'arc *(Maclura pomifera)*.

The bois d'arc, or osage orange, is a fast-growing thorny tree that can be kept clipped to be grown as a hedge. It was popular for hedgerows until barbed wire was introduced. Fruits supply decorative fresh pods.

Giant reed *(Arundo donax)*.

This species lends itself to high natural fencing and decorative material. When freezing occurs, the old stalks remain and the new spring growth is rapid.

Macartney rose *(Rosa bracteata)*.

This rose bush is impenetrable, reaching 10′–20′ high, in mounds. Care is necessary in controlling its growth. In the past, the Macartney rose was used as windbreaks. Foliage and hips are design materials.

Retama *(Parkinsonia aculeata)*.

This small yellow flowering tree, with plumelike leaves, can be untouchable because of its extremely sharp thorns. Foliage and pods are design material.

Cultivating Methods

One way to apply natural grass seeds to small areas is broadcasting with a spreader. Small in size, it is easily handled. Cranked by hand and moved about, this device can spread seeds in 3′ swaths. In existing garden beds, seeds can also be distributed by hand, made to fall in specific areas. In order to grow larger plantings of grasses, as in a plot or a field, the machine process of disking is recommended for preparing the ground. Afterward, the spreader can be adjusted to broadcast seeds wider, in 8′ swaths. It is not difficult to broadcast seeds with a spreader in one to four acres. Since seeds of many species are tiny, it is important that in rolling the field the dirt is applied in a thin cover. Most cool-season flower seeds should be broadcast or planted during late summer and fall. Cool-season grass seeds should be broadcast late in the fall, and warm-season grass seeds in the early spring. Spreaders, which can also be used to fertilize, can be rented or purchased at feed and hardware stores.

The United States Department of Agriculture Soil Conservation Service, the Texas Agricultural Extension Service, the Texas A&M University System, and county agents are on hand to advise the public in methods of cultivating.

CONSERVATION OF NATURALS

Some departments of our state government foster conservation and beautification. Preserving natural vegetation is also the goal of several organizations in the state. Public awareness of the wealth of Texas wildflowers and natural vegetation is being promoted through publications available to the public as part of the various programs.

These government and private organizations present historical, educational, and other interesting facts about the continuing movement in conservation and beautification in Texas. One of the objectives is to provide information as to the availability of native flora. The art of collecting seeds is one of the educational programs offered at Wild Basin in Austin. This knowledge prompts individuals to cultivate their own naturals. Rescuing native and rare plants from the path of bulldozers is an outstanding accomplishment of Operation Plant Rescue in Houston.

Texas Department of Highways and Public Transportation. Since the 1930s, this state agency has been involved with a beautification program. Three pamphlets on native plant life and mowing standards have been developed and published for use by both the public and the Highway Department personnel. This information creates interest and appreciation of the beauty in highway landscaping.

In the 1950s *Native Flora of Texas* was issued to illustrate the abundance of native flora. Information was included on blooming dates of wild flowers, which are being affected by climatic conditions. The blooming stage of species in the warmest regions of the state progresses northward at the rate of about fifteen miles per day. The revised edition of this pamphlet is *Wildflower Manual,* avilable to the public. It emphasizes the established program of protecting and distributing our native flora. The Highway Department distributes wild flower seeds in locations that are barren, the seeds being harvested in areas that have an abundance of a species. Texas highway mowing standards for beautification are explained in the pamphlet *Mowing Standards,* first printed in 1970 and revised in 1984. Mowing standards have been developed to obtain uniform maintenance of highway flora with priorities for safety and appearance. Mowing does not occur until after most of the spring wild flowers and grasses have finished blooming. By keeping these areas unmowed, late blooming varieties are protected and seeds are left to mature.

Texas Department of Agriculture. In 1983, this department initiated an excellent program to promote production and use of native Texas plants. At the present time approximately 85 percent of all landscape plants used in Texas are imported from outside the state, in spite of the fact that Texas has hundreds of beautiful shrubs, vines, trees, and grasses that are naturally adapted to our soil and climate. When used in their areas of adaptation many of these plants require less water and have far fewer problems with pests than do imported varieties. The department began a marketing program to encourage the greater use of these natives for business, home, and government landscaping. The first step taken to market these plants was to publish two booklets: *Texas Native Tree Directory* and *Texas Native Plant Directory.* These are a result of surveys the department conducted of Texas nursery growers to determine the availability of plants that have high merit as landscape material. The two directories contain a list of the wholesale and retail suppliers of native plants as well as a listing by regions of suitable plants, but they do not include descriptive information on the species. A third edition, *Texas Native Tree and Plant Directory*, combines the data from the earlier directories.

National Wildflower Research Center. This organization is dedicated to the preservation, propagation, and use of wild flowers and other native plants in public and private landscapes throughout the United States. A group of concerned citizens from various regions of the country, interested in preserving and promoting naturals for beautification, established this organization in 1982. Co-chairs are Lady Bird Johnson and Helen Hayes. At the National Wildflower Research Center, located along the Colorado River near Austin, experiments are being undertaken to learn how best to propagate and grow wild flowers and native plants. There is a need for additional knowledge of propagation and management before wild flower landscapes can become successful in suitable areas. These native flowers and plants are hardy survivors that contribute to improving our environment. It has been found that wild flowers conserve water and cut maintenance costs of the upkeep of roads and public areas. Naturals can also contribute in beautifying industrial sites and they provide an alternate to the conventional residential and commercial landscaping.

Wild Basin Wilderness. This preserve near Austin was founded in the mid-1970s by citizens of the area. The idea of preserving a portion of the natural beauty, often found within the city limits, was supported by individuals, private organizations, businesses, and the United States Department of the Interior. A preserve was established by buying land in an area known as the Wild Basin of Bee Creek. This wilderness is representative of Texas Hill Country plant life. Many acres are unusual in that nonnative plants do not exist there. This factor is valuable in obtaining the Wild Basin's goal of preserving and protecting a prime example of the habitat. The nonnative species can be aggressive in their displacement of native species, thus reducing a preserve's scientific value. An active educational program for adults and children is in progress, providing an opportunity to learn the geological formation of the Hill Country and to study the common woody plants, grasses, and wild flowers growing in the basin. The seed harvesting program involves collecting seeds of native plants for revegetation and research. The Full Moon Tour is a pleasurable walk to watch the sun set and the moon rise in tranquil and untouched surroundings. Today, within the 200-acre preserve, rare plants that have been in the Wild Basin Wilderness for thousands of years continue to thrive in this protected habitat.

Operation Plant Rescue. The Park People of Houston is the organization responsible for this worthy program relating to plant life. The program relocates plants and trees from land designated for development. Permission from developers is granted to this organization to relocate species that would otherwise be destroyed. Operation Plant Rescue members survey developers' property to evaluate plant materials suitable for future projects. The selection is based upon preserving endangered species and those indigenous to the Houston area. Valuable plants and trees are transplanted in parks, playgrounds, campuses, and other open spaces. The Park People compiled a booklet, *Native and Adapted Trees*, listing trees of lesser known species that individuals are encouraged to plant. Species native to the area usually have a higher survival rate and are recommended for beautification. Also included in the list are those plants and trees that can adapt to local climatic conditions.

Westcave Preserve. A haven of natural vegetation, unusual for the comparatively dry elevations of the Hill Country, is protected by the Westcave Preserve. This preserve is an enchantment for visitors and students, a naturally created terrarium in a lush canyon. Millions of years ago this area was an underground river. Today's formation is the result of erosion that caused the limestone ceiling of a cave to collapse. Cypress trees that are 600 years old border bottomless crystalline pools, shading mosses, ferns, wild flowers, and grasses. The cool moist air, brought about by the cascading creek, springs, and waterfalls, is conducive to the growth of the plant life. There is usually a temperature change of seventeen degrees between the upland areas of the preserve and the canyon floor. The land is owned by the Lower Colorado River Authority and managed by the Westcave Preserve Corporation. Located at the eastern edge of the Edwards Plateau, overlooking the Pedernales River, the 31-acre preserve is off Texas 71, easily accessible from Austin and the surrounding areas.

David Foster. One of the pioneers in introducing new grasses to Texas, Foster, of Uvalde, founded Texas Grasseed Growers in the late 1940s. He was an agronomist with the United States Department of Agriculture Soil Conservation Service and actively engaged in the research and development of native and introduced grasses, such as K.R. bluestem, Kleberg bluestem, Gordo bluestem, and Medio bluestem. In 1949 he broadcast a series of seven radio interviews on this subject while working in San Antonio. The interviews were compiled into a pamphlet entitled *Some Southwestern Pasture Grasses: Seven Interviews on Pasture Grasses with Dave Foster*. Foster's son-in-law Johnny Rambie and his son continue the family interest in grasses, many of which can be decorative and ornamental.

Douglass W. King. In 1912 in San Antonio, King was an early expert on native and naturalized grass seeds. He was responsible for issuing in 1975, with the aid of government agricultural agencies, a booklet titled *Grass Seed*. It has proved to be a successful and informative publication with factual information concerning a variety of grasses. In addition to a description of species, it also includes the value of proper selection according to adaptability to climatic conditions and soil and recommends seeding dates and methods. It contains proof that perennial grasses are much slower to become established than annuals.

Lilypons Water Gardens. This nursery originated in Maryland in 1917 as the Three Springs Fisheries. George Leicester Thomas, Sr., the owner, raised goldfish and grew water lilies. In 1930 the name was changed to Lilypons, in honor of the famous Metropolitan Opera star. During the thirties, water lilies became of great interest to the public. Growing them was fashionable and they were seen in elaborate ponds of the palatial homes of that era. Located in Brookshire, Texas, since 1978, the gardens are cultivating a variety of water plants for beautification. Today, water lilies have again had a recurrence in popularity.

Endangered species often survive along fence lines bordering roadsides. The magnificent cardinal flower, now seen infrequently, still can be found undisturbed, towering between the barbed-wire fences. Motorists attracted to the spectacular color of the mountain pink will find this disappearing flower growing in small patches on gravel lime sites. The beauty of the countryside can continue to be shared and appreciated best if plants are left undisturbed in their natural surroundings. The collection of seeds and naturals can be made from waste and devastated areas. Ornamental plants can be salvaged from properties to be developed. One basic reason for cultivating is to provide seeds for growing and plants for decorating and beautification. In this way, one person can make an immediate contribution to conservation.

Glossary

Achene.	A dry indehiscent, one-seeded fruit, formed from a single female flower.
Acuminate.	Gradually tapering to a tip or apex.
Alternate.	Borne singularly at different levels on the stem or axis.
Annual.	A plant that has a life cycle of one year or less.
Anther.	Pollen-bearing portion of the stamen.
Appendage.	An attached supplementary part.
Awn.	A bristlelike appendage; a hairlike projection in the grass spikelet.
Axil.	The angle between a leaf and the stem on which the leaf is borne.
Axis.	The main stem of a seed head, particularly of a panicle upon which the organs are arranged.
Basal.	Located at the base.
Berry.	A fleshy fruit without a stony layer, usually contains one or more seeds imbedded in the pulpy mass.
Blade.	Expanded portion of a leaf or flower.
Bract.	A modified leaf, subtending an inflorescence or flower.
Bulblet.	A bulblike part.
Bunch grass.	A grass that habitually grows in a tuft.
Calyx.	The outermost whorl in a complete flower; the sepals that are petallike.
Catkin.	A cluster of newborn flowers, usually hanging.
Colony.	A group of plants all of the same species isolated from other stands.
Corolla.	The petals collectively, usually colored; the whorl of showy flower parts.
Culm.	The stem of a grass.
Dehiscent.	Opening spontaneously when ripe.
Deltoid.	Triangular.
Disk.	The head of tubular flowers, as of the sunflowers; the central portion of the head.
Drupe.	A fleshy fruit enclosing one or more seeds, each surrounded by a stony layer.
Drupelet.	A small drupe.
Floret.	A small flower, numbers of which make up a dense inflorescence; in grass, a unit of a spikelet.
Flower.	Plant parts of grasses, trees, and flowers that are reproductive.
Forb.	A herbaceous plant existing in its native habitat, except grasses and grasslike forms.
Glabrous.	Without hairs, smooth.
Herb.	A plant lacking persistent aerial structure, dying back to the earth.
Herbage.	Leaves and stems of a herbaceous plant.
Hip.	Fruit of a rose.
Indehiscent.	Fruits that do not split open to discharge the seeds, remaining closed at maturity.
Inflorescence.	The flowering portion of a shoot; the arrangement of several flowers on a flower or grass shoot.
Lanceolate.	Two or three times as long as broad, flattened, widest in the middle tapering to an apex.

Leaflet.	Separate segment of a compound leaf.
Leaf sheath.	Lower part of a leaf, as in grasses; envelops the stem.
Legume.	A one-celled fruit, usually dehiscent, divided into two valves, along two grooves; the fruit is called a pod.
Ligule.	A hairy appendage at the junction of the leaf sheath and base, existing in grasses.
Node.	Region of the stem, branch, or spikelet axis where the leaf, bracts, or secondary branches emerge.
Ovate.	Egg-shaped, with the broadest end toward the base.
Panicle.	A seed head with a main axis with branches subdivided, open, or spikelike.
Pedicel.	A stalk of single flower; in grass, the stalk of single spikelet.
Peduncle.	A primary flower stalk, supporting a cluster of flowers, later the fruit; in grasses, the stalk of a spikelet cluster.
Perennial.	Growing for more than one year.
Petiole.	A leaf stalk.
Pinnate.	Compound leaf; leaves divided into leaflets along a common petiole.
Pistil.	The reproductive female part of the flower, consisting of the stigmas, ovary, and style.
Pistillate.	Having pistils but no fertile stamens.
Plumose.	Feathery, elongated fine hairs on either side.
Pod.	Any dry dehiscent fruit, frequently applied to legumes, but also applied to other fruits; decorative pod, any dehiscent or indehiscent fruit.
Pollen.	The dustlike substance from the anthers.
Pubescent.	With fine, soft short hairs.
Raceme.	Inflorescence with a main axis bearing stalked flowers opening from the base upward.
Rachis.	The axis of a pinnately compound leaf; the axis of an inflorescence.
Rootstock.	A rhizome or an elongated underground stem; a rhizomelike structure.
Rosette.	A round cluster of leaves radiating from the stem, all at nearly the same level.
Samara.	An indehiscent winged fruit, such as that of a maple.
Sepal.	One of the members of a calyx, petallike.
Sessile.	Without a petiole or stalk.
Spike.	In flowers, an unbranched inflorescence with flowers unstalked and opening upward from the base; in grasses an unbranched seed head in which the spikelets are sessile on a rachis.
Spikelet.	In grasses, a secondary spike consisting of two glumes (chaffy bracts) and one or more florets.
Stamen.	The male organ of the flower that produces pollen.
Staminate.	Having stamens only, no pistils.
Whorl.	A circular arrangement of similar parts radiating from a node.

References

Agricultural Research Service of the United States Department of Agriculture. *Common Weeds of the United States*. New York: Dover Publications, 1971.

Ajilvsgi, Geyata. *Wildflowers of Texas*. Bryan, Tex.: Shearer Publishing, 1984.

Berry, Edward Wilbur. *Tree Ancestors*. Baltimore: Waverly Press, 1923.

Correll, Donovan S., and Marshall C. Johnston. *Manual of the Vascular Plants of Texas*. Renner: Texas Research Foundation, 1970; reprint, Dallas: University of Texas at Dallas, 1979.

Flower Designs in Japan. Tokyo: Rikuyosha, 1982.

Gould, Frank W. *The Grasses of Texas*. College Station: Texas A&M University Press, 1975.

———. *Texas Plants: A Checklist and Ecological Summary*. MP-585. College Station: Texas Agricultural Experiment Station, 1969.

Gray, Asa. *Gray's School and Field Book of Botany*. New York: Ivison, Blakeman, Taylor, 1876.

Greene, Wilhelmina F., and Hugo L. Blomquist. *Flowers of the South*. Chapel Hill: University of North Carolina Press, 1953.

Hitchcock, Albert Spear. *Manual of the Grasses of the United States*. Washington, D.C.: U.S. Government Printing Office, 1935.

Hora, Bayard. *The Oxford Encyclopedia of Trees of the World*. Oxford: Oxford University Press, 1981.

Hughes, Melody. *Wildflower Manual*. Austin: State Department of Highways and Public Transportation Maintenance Divisions, 1981.

King, Ronald. *Botanical Illustrations*. New York: Clarkson N. Potter, 1978.

Loughmiller, Campbell and Lynne. *Texas Wildflowers*. Austin: University of Texas Press, 1984.

Lynch, Brother Daniel, C.S.C. *Native and Naturalized Woody Plants of Austin and the Hill Country*. Austin: Saint Edward's University, 1981.

Niehaus, Theodore F. *A Field Guide to Southwestern and Texas Wildflowers*. Boston: Houghton Mifflin Co., 1984.

Peterson, Lee. *A Field Guide to Edible Wild Plants of Eastern and Central North America*. Boston: Houghton Mifflin Co., 1979.

Phillips Petroleum Co. *Pasture and Range Plants*. Bartlesville, Okla., 1963.

Ragsdale, B. J., and G. O. Hoffman. *Know Your Grasses*. College Station: Texas Agricultural Extension Service, Texas A&M University System, 1976.

Rickett, Harold William. *Wild Flowers of the United States*. Vol. 1. Publication of the New York Botanical Garden. New York: McGraw-Hill Book Co., 1966.

Scruggs, Gross R. *Gardening in the Southwest*. Dallas: Southwest Press, 1932; reprint, Garden City, N.Y.: Doubleday and Co., 1952.

Soil Conservation Service, United States Department of Agriculture. *100 Native Forage Grasses in 11 Southern States*. Agriculture Handbook no. 389. Washington, D.C.: U.S. Government Printing Office, 1971.

Taylor, Kathryn S., and Stephen F. Hamblin. *Handbook of Wild Flower Cultivation*. New York: Macmillan Publishing Co., 1963.

Taylor, Norman. *A Guide to the Wild Flowers*. Garden City, N.Y.: Garden City Publishing Co., 1928.

Texas Department of Agriculture. *Texas Native Tree Directory 1984*. Austin, 1984.

———. *Texas Native Plant Directory 1984*. Austin, 1984.

———. *Texas Native Tree and Plant Directory*. Austin, 1986.

Tharp, Benjamin Carroll. *Texas Range Grass*. Austin: University of Texas Press, 1952.

Turner, B. L. *The Legumes of Texas*. Austin: University of Texas Press, 1959.

Verrill, Alpheus Hyatt. *Wonder Plants and Plant Wonders*. New York, London: D. Appleton Co., Century Co., 1939.

Vines, Robert A. *Trees, Shrubs, and Woody Vines of the Southwest*. Austin: University of Texas Press, 1960.

Wasowski, Sally, and Julie E. Ryan. *Landscaping with Native Texas Plants*. Austin: Texas Monthly Press, 1985.

Whitehouse, Eula. *Texas Flowers in Natural Colors*. Austin: Privately published, 1936; reprinted, Dallas: Dallas County Audubon Society, 1967.

Wills, Mary Motz, and Howard S. Irwin. *Roadside Flowers of Texas*. Austin: University of Texas Press, 1961.

Index

Achillea millefolium, 109
Aesculus pavia, 64
agarita, 34, 111, 113, 114
Agrostis hiemalis, 110
Ailanthus altissima, 54
alamo tree, 62
alamo vine, 72, 102, 105, 106, 112
Allium
    canadense, 42
    drummondii, 42
Alopecurus carolinianus, 110
Ampelopsis arborea, 78
Andropogon, 34
    glomeratus, 110
    ternarius, 34, 110
    virginicus, 110
Aristida pururea, 18, 112
Arundo donox, 26, 111, 114
ash tree, 54
Avena fatua, 16, 110
    var. *sativa*, 16, 110

bachelor button, 18, 40
bagpod sesbania, 58, 94, 106, 110
balloon vine, 112
Baptisia sphaerocarpa, 111
barbas de chivato, 74
basket flower, 82, 109
beard grass, 34
bear grass, 96
beauty-berry, American, 113
Bengal grass, 14
bent grass, winter, 46, 110
Berberis trifoliolata, 111, 113, 114
Berchemia scandens, 80
bergamot, wild, 48, 109
bergamot orange tree, 48
black-eyed Susan, 46, 52, 109
black Sampson, 109
bluebell, 109
bluebonnet, 2
bluestem, 32, 34, 60, 105
    big, 2, 20, 32
    broom sedge, 102, 110
    bushy, 110
    Gordo, 116
    K. R., 116
    Kleberg, 116
    little, 2, 20, 32, 34, 103, 110, 112
    Medio, 116
    splitbeard, 2, 22, 34, 60, 110
bois d'arc, 3, 56, 102, 106, 114
bristle grass
    green, 14, 110, 113
    southwest, 24, 110
brome, Japanese, 28, 110
Bromus japonicus, 28, 102, 110

broomweed, 28, 102
    common, 90, 110
brown-eyed Susan, 109
buckeye, 106
    Mexican, 8
    red, 64, 80, 103
    scarlet, 64
bulrush, great, 111
buttonball tree, 66
buttonwood tree, 66

Callicarpa americana, 113
Campsis radicans, 76, 113
candelilla, 2
cane
    Georgia, 26
    giant, 26, 68
cardinal flower, 117
Cardiospermum halicacabum, 112
carrot, wild, 20
castor-oil plant, 105, 106
cattail, 105, 106
    broadleaf, 96
    narrowleaf, 96, 111
cedar, mountain, 84
Centaurea americana, 109
Chasmanthium latifolium, 22, 110, 113
chess, Japanese, 28
chili, red, 78
chinaberry, 3, 12, 60, 106, 113
China tree, wild, 52
cinnamon sticks, 78
Clematis drummondii, 74, 112
Cocculus carolinus, 84
coffee bean, 94
coneflower, 46
    purple, 109
copal tree, 54
coralvine, 56
coreopsis, 32, 109
Coreopsis
    basalis, 109
    grandiflora, 109
    tinctoria, 109
cotton, 74
cottonwood
    eastern, 62, 113
    southern, 62
croton, woolly, 88, 110, 111, 113
Croton capitatus, 88, 110, 111, 113
    var. *albinoides*, 88
    var. *lindheimeri*, 88
Cyperus esculentus, 111
cypress tree, 116

daisy, gerbera, 30
Delphinium carolinianum, 109
devil's-claw, 40, 102
dill, wild, 32, 109
Diospyros texana, 113
dock, 92, 102, 103, 105
    curly, 3, 92, 110
dodder, 102
doveweed, 88, 110
duck acorn, 44

Echinacea
    angustifolia, 109
    sanguinea, 109
Elymus
    canadensis, 6, 8, 110
    virginicus, 6, 110
Equisetum, 98
    hyemale, 111
    laevigatum, 111
Eragrostis curvula, 110
Eryngium
    heterophyllum, 109
    leavenworthii, 109
    yuccifolium, 109, 113
eryngo
    Leavenworth, 18, 34, 102, 109
    yucca-leaf, 109, 113
euphorbia, wax, 2
Eustoma grandiflorum, 109

fern, maidenhair, 38
firecracker plant, 64
forsythia, 92
foxtail, 46, 102. *See also* millet
    Carolina, 110

gama grass, eastern, 102, 110
gay feather, 109
gentian, prairie, 109
goat beard, 74
goatweed, 88, 102, 110
goldenrod, 109
gomphrena, 18
gourd
    buffalo, 50
    Indian, 50
greenbrier, 102, 113
Gutierrezia
    dracunculoides, 90, 102, 110
    sarothrae, 110

Helianthus
    annuus, 109, 113
    maximiliani, 113
hogwort, 88
holly, yaupon, 113

honeysuckle, 102, 105
   Chinese, 82
   coral, 112
   Japanese, 34, 82, 112, 113
   southern, 82
   white, 82, 112, 113
horseapple, 3, 56
horsebean, 58
horsemint, 48, 102
   lemon, 48, 109, 113
   purple, 48, 109, 113
   yellow, 109
horsenettle, Carolina, 50
horsetail, 98, 102, 111
hydrangea, 54

Ilex vomitoria, 113
Indian grass, 2, 20, 32, 102, 110
Indian lilac, 60
indigo, wild, 111
Ipomoea sinuata, 72, 112
ironweed, western, 109

jaboncillo, 52
jack-in-the-pulpit, 2
Jerusalem thorn, 58
Johnson grass, 12, 30, 102
jujube tree, 80
juncus, 107
Juncus
   effusus, 111
   marginatus, 110
   validus, 111
juniper, 2
   Ashe, 84

larkspur, Carolina, 109
liatris, 34, 48, 109
Liatris
   elegans, 109
   punctata, 109
lily
   Nerine, 30
   rubrum, 56
   swamp, 2
   yellow matchless, 92
Limonium nashii, 111
live oak, 113
Lolium perenne, 10, 110, 112
Lonicera
   albiflora, 112
   japonica, 82, 112
   sempervirens, 112
lotus
   American, 2, 14, 44, 74, 102, 107, 111
   yellow, 44
love-in-the-mist, 74

Maclura pomifera, 56, 114
   var. *inermis*, 56
magnolia, 16, 18, 20
mayapple, 2
Melia azedarach, 60
   var. *umbraculiformis*, 60
Mexican hat, 2, 40, 102, 106, 111
millet
   foxtail, 14, 20, 56, 103, 110, 113
   Italian, 14
Monarda
   citriodora, 48, 109, 113
   fistulosa, 109
   pectinata, 109
   punctata, 48, 109
moonseed
   Carolina, 84
   red-berried, 84
Muhlenbergia capillaris, 110
muhly, hairy-awn, 34, 110
mullein, 20, 102
   common, 109
   great, 109, 111

narcissus, China shine, 98
Nelumbo lutea, 44, 111
nightshade, silverleaf, 50
nut sedge, yellow, 111

oak, sawtooth, 113
oat
   common, 16, 110
   wild, 16, 102, 110
old-man's-beard, 22, 74, 102, 105, 112
onion, wild, 42, 96, 102
orchid, yellow lady's slipper, 2
osage orange, 40, 56, 114

palm, dwarf, 68
palmetto, dwarf, 68, 111
paloverde, 58
Papaver rhoeas, 109
Parkinsonia aculeata, 58, 114
parsley, prairie, 109
Passiflora
   caerulea, 112
   incarnata, 112, 113
passionflower, 102, 112, 113
pepper vine, 78, 102, 105, 106, 113
persimmon, Texas, 113
Phytolacca americana, 113
pine, 34
   pinyon, 2
   ponderosa, 2
pink, mountain, 117
pitcher plant, 111
plains beebalm, 109

plane tree, American, 66
Platanus occidentalis, 66
plum, wild, 113
pokeberry, 113
Polypogon monspeliensis, 111
Polytaenia nuttallii, 109
poplar
   black, 62
   necklace, 62
   water, 62
Populus deltoides, 62
   × *canadensis*, 62
poppy
   corn, 109
   red, 109
   wild, 48, 96
prairie wedgescale, 110
pride-of-India, 60
Prunus americana, 113
purpletop, 2, 30, 34, 48, 102, 110
   Chapman, 30

rabbit-foot grass, 111
Ratibida
   columnaris, 40, 111
   peduncularis, 40
      var. *tagetes*, 40
rattan vine, 34, 64, 80, 102, 105, 106, 113
rattlebox, Drummond, 94
ray grass, 10
reed, giant, 26, 68, 102, 105, 111, 114
retama, 58, 102, 114
Rhus
   copallina var. *lanceolata*, 113
   glabra, 113
Rhynchospora corniculata, 111
rice, 44, 82
Rosa bracteata, 38, 114
rose
   Macartney, 38, 102, 106, 114
   prairie, 38
   wild white, 38
Rudbeckia
   amplexicaulis, 46
   hirta, 46, 109
   serotina, 109
Rumex crispus, 92, 110
rush, 106
   common, 111
   horned beak, 8, 111
   roundhead, 111
   scouring, 98
   shore, 82, 96, 102, 110
ryegrass, perennial, 6, 10, 110, 112

Sabal minor, 68, 111
salt-cedar, 2
Sapindus drummondii, 52
sarracenia, 2, 111
Sarracenia alata, 30, 111
Schizachyrium scoparium, 20, 110, 112
Scirpus validus, 111
sea lavender, 111
seaoats, inland, 22, 110
Sesbania vesicaria, 94, 110
Setaria
   italica, 14, 110, 113
   scheelei, 24, 110
   viridis, 14, 110, 113
side oats grama, 2
smut grass, 102
snailseed, Carolina, 84, 113
snakeweed, broom, 110
soapberry, 102, 106
   western, 52, 113
soap-plant, Indian, 52
Solanum
   carolinense, 50
   elaeagnifolium, 50
Solidago
   altissima, 109
   radula, 109
Sorghastrum nutans, 32, 110
Sorghum halepense, 12
Sphenopholis obtusata, 110
sumac
   Chinese, 54, 102
   prairie flame-leaf, 113
   smooth, 113
sunflower, 12, 52, 74
   common, 109, 113
   Maximilian, 113
supplejack, Alabama, 80
switch grass, 2, 30, 32
sycamore, 34, 52, 54, 66, 102, 113
   American, 34, 52, 54, 66

tamarisk, 2, 16
Texas virgin's bower, 74
thimbleflower, 40
thistle
   Mexican, 32, 109
   Russian, 3
three-awn, purple, 18, 112
timothy, 20
tree of heaven, 54, 113
Tridens flavus, 30, 110
   var. *chapmanii*, 30
Tripsacum dactyloides, 110
trompillo, 50
Tulip Kees Nelis, 92
tumbleweed, 3

trumpet creeper, 76, 102, 105, 113
trumpet vine, 58, 76, 82, 102, 105
turkey vine, 78, 102
Typha
   angustifolia, 96, 111
   latifolia, 96

uniola, broadleaf, 22, 110, 113
Uniola paniculata, 22

Verbascum thapsus, 109, 111
Vernonia baldwinii, 109
Victoria amazonia, 44

water lily, 107, 117
   royal, 44
weeping love grass, 110
wild rye
   Canada, 2, 6, 8, 102, 110
   nodding, 8
   Virginia, 2, 6, 8, 110
woodrose, 72, 102

yarrow, 109
yucca, 2